Natural Farming and Soil Regeneration

Techniques for Sustainable Agronomic Systems

Written by

Avimanyu Palit

Mayukh Bhattacharyya

Dr. Suddhasuchi Das

2025

SPI Publications

Published by **SPI Publications**, www.spipublications.in

SPI, the **SPI logo**, and **Split Poetry India** are trademarks of **SPI Publications**, or its affiliates.

ISBN-13: 978-93-49860-65-0

First Edition 2025

SPI Publications

Corporate & Editorial Office

117/2, Sector 37, Khandsa Road,
Gurgaon, Haryana 122 001
Phone: +91 98355 52940
Email: contact@spipublications.in
Website: www.spipublications.in

Processed and Printed in India

Preface

In an era where industrial agriculture has reached its productivity peak at the cost of soil degradation, biodiversity loss, and farmer distress, the need for a transformative shift in agronomic practice has never been more urgent. This book, *Natural Farming and Soil Regeneration: Techniques for Sustainable Agronomic Systems*, emerges from a growing consensus among scientists, farmers, and policy-makers that sustainable food production must begin with the soil—and be guided by nature.

Rooted in rigorous scientific understanding and enriched by indigenous wisdom, this book is the outcome of collaborative research, field experimentation, and hands-on experience with regenerative natural farming systems. It offers readers a comprehensive exploration of natural farming as both a philosophy and a science—bridging traditional ecological knowledge with contemporary agronomic principles.

We have endeavored to present this work not merely as a critique of conventional and organic systems but as a constructive manual for transitioning toward input-free, biodiversity-rich, and ecologically resilient farming methods. From the microbiology of living soils to water conservation, from crop diversity and pest regulation to the economic implications of zero-budget natural farming, this volume integrates theoretical insight with actionable guidance.

The chapters are structured to support farmers, students, researchers, and extension workers alike. Each section builds upon the foundational concepts of soil health and ecological balance, providing practical tools for implementation in diverse agro-climatic contexts. We also examine emerging trends such as climate-resilient agriculture, polyculture integration, and the role of natural farming in urban and peri-urban environments.

We express our deepest gratitude to the farming communities whose indigenous knowledge and lived experiences have inspired many of the ideas in this book. Their commitment to the land and resilience in the face of agrarian challenges remain the cornerstone of our motivation.

It is our sincere hope that this book will contribute to a new paradigm of agronomy—one that respects the interconnectedness of soil, plant, animal, and human health—and that it serves as a trusted reference for those committed to cultivating both the earth and the ethos of sustainability.

Avimanyu Palit
Mayukh Bhattacharyya
Dr. Suddhasuchi Das
2025

ICARDA
Science for resilient livelihoods in dry areas

Foreword

The challenges confronting agriculture today — soil degradation, loss of biodiversity, excessive dependence on external inputs, and growing climate vulnerabilities — demand transformative action in the way we produce food. In our pursuit of solutions that are both scientifically robust and ecologically responsible, natural farming and soil regeneration have emerged as vital pathways for restoring the balance between productivity, sustainability, and resilience.

It is within this context that ***Natural Farming and Soil Regeneration: Techniques for Sustainable Agronomic Systems*** offers a timely and important contribution. Co-authored by Mr. Avimanyu Palit, Mr. Mayukh Bhattacharyya, and Dr. Suddhasuchi Das, this book presents rigorous scientific analysis with practical, field-tested approaches, drawing strength from both contemporary research and enduring indigenous knowledge systems.

Rather than presenting natural farming as a return to the past, the authors position it as a dynamic and evolving system rooted in soil biology and ecological principles. Through its exploration of zero-budget natural farming, ecological intensification, and the relevance of traditional knowledge in modern agriculture, the book presents a comprehensive and forward-looking perspective on regenerative agriculture. Its emphasis on input-free and locally adapted systems demonstrates not only their environmental benefits but also their economic viability for both smallholders and larger farming enterprises.

Particularly noteworthy is the book's commitment to practical application. The models and case studies it presents are grounded in real-world experiences across diverse agro-climatic zones, making the volume an invaluable resource for students, researchers, extension professionals, and progressive farmers alike. Readers will find both theoretical depth and hands-on insights—an essential combination for those seeking meaningful change on the ground.

As someone deeply engaged in the interface of agricultural science and sustainable development, I commend this work for its clarity, relevance, and vision. More than just a reference, this book is a compelling call to reimagine agriculture as a regenerative, inclusive, and life-enhancing endeavour.

I am confident that this volume will inspire and inform a wide audience, helping to chart a more sustainable, resilient, and soil-centered future for farming.

Dr. Shiv Kumar Agrawal
Regional Coordinator, South Asia & China
Head, Food Legume Research Platform (FLRP), ICARDA

Office Block-C, NASC Complex | DPS Marg, Pusa | New Delhi-110012, India
Tel:+91-11-25847505

icarda.org
International Center for Agricultural Research in the Dry Areas

cgiar.org
A CGIAR Research Center

Index

Chapter 1: Decoding Natural Farming: Principles and Practices

1.1 What is Natural Farming?

Natural farming is a holistic approach to agriculture that emphasizes working in harmony with nature rather than manipulating it through synthetic chemicals and heavy machinery. Unlike conventional farming, which relies on chemical fertilizers, pesticides, and intensive irrigation, natural farming fosters biodiversity, improves soil health, and enhances the natural balance of ecosystems.

At its core, natural farming is guided by the principle that nature, when left undisturbed, has an inherent ability to sustain and regenerate itself. By mimicking natural processes, farmers can cultivate healthy crops without depleting resources or harming the environment.

This method stands apart from both **conventional** and **organic farming**:

- **Conventional Farming**: Relies on synthetic fertilizers, pesticides, and genetically modified seeds to maximize yield.
- **Organic Farming**: Avoids synthetic chemicals but still depends on external inputs like compost, manure, and bio-pesticides.
- **Natural Farming**: Requires no external inputs. It depends on natural soil fertility, native biodiversity, and ecological cycles to sustain crop production.

The Core Principles of Natural Farming:

1. **Minimal Human Intervention** – Let nature take its course with as little disruption as possible.
2. **No Synthetic Chemicals** – Avoid the use of artificial fertilizers and pesticides.
3. **Living Soil Approach** – Foster a soil rich in microorganisms and organic matter.
4. **Diversity in Cultivation** – Encourage polyculture and companion planting to mimic natural ecosystems.
5. **Water Conservation** – Utilize rainwater harvesting, mulch, and natural irrigation methods.

Natural farming is not just an agricultural technique - it is a **philosophy**, a **science**, and a **way of life** that aligns with sustainable development and environmental conservation.

1.2 The Philosophical Foundations of Natural Farming

The principles of natural farming are deeply rooted in traditional agricultural wisdom and ecological balance. Over centuries, many indigenous farming systems around the world have followed a similar approach, prioritizing natural cycles and resource conservation.

Influential Thinkers and Movements

- **Masanobu Fukuoka (Japan)**

  Fukuoka, the father of "Do-Nothing Farming," revolutionized agriculture with his book *The One-Straw Revolution* (1975). His philosophy is based on four principles:

  1. No tilling
  2. No chemical fertilizers
  3. No pesticides
  4. No weeding

  He demonstrated how natural farming yields could match or exceed those of conventional farms while improving soil fertility over time.

- **Subhash Palekar (India)**

  Palekar developed **Zero Budget Natural Farming (ZBNF)**, a system that enables farmers to grow crops without expensive chemical inputs. His method promotes the use of indigenous cow dung and urine-based fertilizers like **Jeevamrit** and **Beejamrit**, which enhance soil microbes and plant nutrition.

- **Rudolf Steiner (Austria)**

  The founder of **Biodynamic Farming**, Steiner emphasized the spiritual and cosmic forces affecting plant growth, integrating lunar cycles, composting techniques, and holistic farm management.

- **Bill Mollison & David Holmgren (Australia)**

  The pioneers of **Permaculture**, they promoted sustainable farming through design principles that mimic natural ecosystems. Their system integrates water harvesting, agroforestry, and multi-functional landscapes.

Natural Farming as a Way of Life

Natural farming is more than just growing food—it is a lifestyle that aligns with the rhythms of nature. It encourages simplicity, mindfulness, and deep respect for the earth. Farmers practicing this approach often see themselves as caretakers rather than controllers of the land.

1.3 The Science Behind Natural Farming

While natural farming is deeply philosophical, it is also grounded in science. The success of natural farming is largely due to its ability to **enhance soil fertility, promote biodiversity, and improve water retention.**

1.3.1 Soil Microbiology: The Foundation of Life

Healthy soil is **alive**, teeming with beneficial microorganisms like bacteria, fungi, nematodes, and earthworms. These organisms break down organic matter, fix nitrogen, and enhance nutrient absorption for plants.

- **Mycorrhizal Fungi** form symbiotic relationships with plant roots, increasing their ability to absorb water and nutrients.
- **Nitrogen-Fixing Bacteria** (such as Rhizobium) naturally enrich the soil by converting atmospheric nitrogen into a plant-usable form.
- **Decomposers** (earthworms, microbes) break down dead organic material, creating humus-rich soil that retains moisture and nutrients.

By avoiding synthetic fertilizers and pesticides, natural farming **nurtures** this delicate web of life instead of disrupting it.

1.3.2 Plant Resilience and Pest Control

In conventional farming, pests and diseases are controlled with chemical pesticides, but in natural farming, the **ecosystem itself** acts as a defense system.

- **Companion Planting**: Certain plants naturally repel pests or attract beneficial insects. For example, marigolds deter nematodes, while basil enhances the growth of tomatoes.
- **Predator Insects**: Encouraging natural predators like ladybugs (which eat aphids) and birds (which eat caterpillars) reduces pest populations naturally.
- **Mulching & Soil Health**: A well-mulched field with diverse plant life discourages harmful pests while supporting beneficial microbes.

1.3.3 Water Conservation & Climate Resilience

One of the biggest advantages of natural farming is its ability to **retain water and resist drought**.

- **Mulching**: A layer of organic mulch reduces evaporation and keeps the soil cool.
- **Deep Root Systems**: Plants grown in healthy, undisturbed soil develop stronger roots that can access deeper water reserves.
- **Agroforestry & Polyculture**: Trees and multiple crops grown together reduce soil erosion and maintain moisture levels.

These techniques make natural farming highly **resilient to climate change**, ensuring stable yields even in extreme weather conditions.

1.4 Why Natural Farming Matters

Natural farming is gaining momentum as a sustainable alternative to chemical-based agriculture. With growing concerns over soil degradation, water shortages, and climate change, it offers a **scalable, cost-effective, and environmentally friendly** way to produce food.

Benefits of Natural Farming:

✅ **Healthier Food** – Free from chemical residues and rich in nutrients.
✅ **Environmental Protection** – Reduces pollution, conserves water, and restores biodiversity.
✅ **Economic Sustainability** – Cuts farming costs by eliminating expensive inputs.
✅ **Climate Resilience** - Builds stronger soil that can withstand extreme weather.

As the world searches for solutions to food security and environmental crises, **natural farming presents a viable path forward**—one that nourishes the earth, the farmer, and the consumer alike.

Conclusion: The Journey Ahead

Understanding natural farming is the first step towards adopting it. This book will guide you through the **principles, techniques, and real-world applications** of natural farming, showing how anyone - whether a small-scale farmer, an urban gardener, or a large landowner—can cultivate food in harmony with nature.

Chapter 2: The Science of Soil and Ecosystem Balance

(Understanding the Biological, Chemical, and Ecological Foundations of Natural Farming)

2.1 The Living Soil: The Foundation of Natural Farming

Soil is more than just dirt - it is a complex, **living ecosystem** that supports all life on Earth. Healthy soil is teeming with microorganisms, fungi, earthworms, and organic matter that contribute to plant health and environmental balance. In natural farming, soil is treated as a **living entity**, not merely a medium for plant growth.

Unlike conventional farming, which often depletes soil fertility through excessive tilling, monocropping, and chemical inputs, **natural farming enhances soil health by encouraging biodiversity and biological activity.**

2.1.1 Components of Healthy Soil

A fertile soil ecosystem consists of four primary components:

1. **Minerals (45%)** – Includes sand, silt, and clay that provide structure and nutrients.
2. **Organic Matter (5%)** – Decayed plant and animal material that nourishes the soil.
3. **Water (25%)** – Essential for nutrient transport and microbial life.
4. **Air (25%)** – Provides oxygen for root and microbial respiration.

This balance is crucial for sustaining life. If any of these elements are disrupted, plant growth and soil fertility suffer.

2.2 Soil Microbiology: The Hidden Workforce Beneath Our Feet

Beneath every natural farm, billions of microorganisms—bacteria, fungi, protozoa, and nematodes - work tirelessly to recycle nutrients, decompose organic matter, and support plant growth.

2.2.1 Key Soil Microorganisms and Their Roles

Mycorrhizal Fungi:

- Form a symbiotic relationship with plant roots, extending their reach to absorb water and nutrients.
- Help break down complex minerals into forms that plants can use.

Nitrogen-Fixing Bacteria (e.g., *Rhizobium* and *Azotobacter*):

- Convert atmospheric nitrogen into forms that plants can absorb.

- Essential for legume crops like beans and peas.

Decomposers (Fungi & Actinomycetes):

- Break down organic material, creating **humus**, a rich, nutrient-dense component of soil.

- Improve soil structure and water retention.

Earthworms & Soil Fauna:

- Improve soil aeration by tunneling through the earth.

- Convert organic material into nutrient-rich **vermicompost**.

By maintaining a **chemical-free environment**, natural farming allows these microorganisms to thrive, ensuring the long-term fertility and health of the soil.

2.3 Soil Nutrients: Feeding Plants the Natural Way

Plants require **macronutrients** and **micronutrients** to grow. In conventional farming, synthetic fertilizers provide these nutrients artificially, often leading to soil degradation over time. **Natural farming, on the other hand, relies on soil microbes and organic matter to deliver nutrients naturally.**

2.3.1 Macronutrients (Needed in Large Quantities)

- **Nitrogen (N):** Promotes leaf and stem growth. Found in compost, cow dung, and leguminous plant residues.

- **Phosphorus (P):** Encourages root development. Found in bone meal, rock phosphate, and composted manure.

- **Potassium (K):** Enhances flower and fruit production. Found in wood ash, banana peels, and biochar.

2.3.2 Micronutrients (Needed in Small Quantities but Essential)

- **Calcium (Ca):** Strengthens plant cell walls.

- **Magnesium (Mg):** Key component of chlorophyll, helping with photosynthesis.

- **Zinc (Zn), Copper (Cu), and Iron (Fe):** Support enzyme function and plant metabolism.

2.3.3 The Role of Organic Matter in Nutrient Cycling

When organic matter (like compost, decomposing plant material, or animal manure) is added to soil, **microorganisms break it down into essential nutrients** that plants can absorb. This process, known as **nutrient cycling**, eliminates the need for synthetic fertilizers.

2.4 The Role of Soil Structure and Mulching in Natural Farming

2.4.1 Soil Structure: Why It Matters

Healthy soil has a **loose, crumbly texture**, allowing roots to penetrate easily and absorb nutrients. Over-tilling in conventional farming **destroys soil structure**, making it compacted and less able to hold water.

Natural farming **protects soil structure** by:
✓**Avoiding deep tillage** – Instead of plowing, natural farmers use cover crops and mulching.
✓**Encouraging organic matter accumulation** – Plant residues decompose naturally, improving soil health.

2.4.2 Mulching: The Natural Blanket for Soil Health

Mulching - covering the soil with organic materials like straw, leaves, or dry grass - offers multiple benefits:
Prevents soil erosion by reducing wind and water impact.
Retains moisture, reducing the need for irrigation.
Regulates soil temperature, keeping roots cool in summer and warm in winter.
Suppresses weeds, reducing competition for nutrients.

Mulching also **provides food for soil organisms**, enhancing biological activity and nutrient availability.

2.5 The Ecosystem Balance: Working with Nature, Not Against It

A successful natural farm is **not just a farm - it is an ecosystem** where plants, animals, and microorganisms exist in harmony.

2.5.1 The Importance of Biodiversity

In monoculture farming, growing only one crop depletes specific nutrients from the soil and increases vulnerability to pests. In contrast, **natural farming promotes diversity**, creating a balanced ecosystem.

Some key biodiversity strategies include:
Companion Planting – Growing plants that support each other (e.g., corn, beans, and squash).
Agroforestry – Integrating trees with crops to improve soil health.
Encouraging Natural Predators – Birds, frogs, and beneficial insects (like ladybugs) help control pests naturally.

2.5.2 Pest and Disease Control Through Ecosystem Management

Instead of chemical pesticides, natural farming relies on:
Biological pest control – Encouraging natural predators to control harmful insects.
Trap crops – Planting certain crops that attract pests away from the main crops.
Homemade natural repellents – Neem oil, garlic spray, and cow urine solutions.

2.6 Water Conservation: Keeping the Soil Hydrated Naturally

Water is a precious resource, and natural farming focuses on **efficient water use**. Key techniques include:

Rainwater Harvesting – Collecting and storing rainwater for irrigation.
Mulching & Cover Crops – Reducing evaporation and improving water retention.
Swales & Contour Farming – Preventing runoff and allowing water to seep into the soil.
Deep Root Systems – Encouraging plants to develop deep roots to access underground moisture.

By using these strategies, natural farms **require less irrigation** and remain productive even in drought conditions.

Conclusion: Soil Health = Farm Health

The **science of soil and ecosystem balance** is the foundation of natural farming. By focusing on soil microbiology, organic matter, biodiversity, and water conservation, farmers can grow crops sustainably **without harming the environment**.

Key Takeaways from This Chapter:

✓**Healthy soil is a living ecosystem** full of beneficial microbes.
✓**Avoiding synthetic chemicals** preserves soil fertility and plant health.
✓**Mulching, cover crops, and composting** naturally enrich the soil.
✓**Ecosystem diversity** helps prevent pests and diseases.
✓**Water conservation** ensures long-term farm sustainability.

By **understanding and respecting soil science**, farmers can cultivate thriving crops while regenerating the earth - a win for both nature and humanity.

Chapter 3: Regenerative vs. Sustainable Agriculture

(Understanding the Differences and Their Role in the Future of Farming)

3.1 Introduction: Why Agriculture Needs to Change

The world is facing an agricultural crisis. Decades of industrial farming have degraded soil, polluted water sources, and contributed to climate change. As a result, there is growing interest in alternative approaches to farming that prioritize environmental health, food security, and long-term sustainability.

Two key approaches that have gained traction are **sustainable agriculture** and **regenerative agriculture**. While both aim to reduce harm to the environment, regenerative agriculture goes one step further by actively **restoring and improving** natural ecosystems.

This chapter explores the differences between **sustainable and regenerative agriculture**, their principles, and why regenerative farming is the future of truly resilient food production.

3.2 What is Sustainable Agriculture?

Sustainable agriculture focuses on **minimizing environmental damage** while ensuring food production for future generations. The goal is to **maintain soil fertility, conserve water, and reduce pollution**, but not necessarily to improve degraded ecosystems.

3.2.1 Principles of Sustainable Agriculture

1. **Resource Conservation** – Using water, soil, and energy efficiently to prevent depletion.
2. **Chemical Reduction** – Reducing or eliminating synthetic fertilizers and pesticides to minimize environmental impact.
3. **Biodiversity Preservation** – Encouraging crop diversity and maintaining natural habitats for wildlife.
4. **Economic Viability** – Ensuring farming remains profitable without exploiting natural resources.
5. **Social Responsibility** – Supporting fair labor practices and local food systems.

Sustainable agriculture **focuses on maintaining the status quo** by preventing further environmental degradation. However, it does not always **actively rebuild** damaged ecosystems or restore soil health.

3.3 What is Regenerative Agriculture?

Regenerative agriculture **goes beyond sustainability** by actively improving soil, water, and biodiversity. Instead of simply minimizing harm, regenerative farming **revitalizes ecosystems**, making them more resilient and productive over time.

3.3.1 Principles of Regenerative Agriculture

1. **Soil Regeneration** – Restoring soil health through composting, cover cropping, and reduced tillage.
2. **Carbon Sequestration** – Using farming practices that capture carbon from the atmosphere and store it in soil.
3. **Biodiversity Enhancement** – Encouraging diverse plant and animal life to create a balanced farm ecosystem.
4. **Holistic Land Management** – Integrating livestock, crops, and forests to mimic natural ecosystems.
5. **Water Cycle Restoration** – Improving water retention through mulching, agroforestry, and no-till farming.

Regenerative farming focuses on **healing the land** while producing food, making it a **more advanced and effective** approach than sustainable farming.

3.4 Key Differences Between Sustainable and Regenerative Agriculture

Aspect	**Sustainable Agriculture**	**Regenerative Agriculture**
Main Goal	Reduce environmental harm	Restore and improve ecosystems
Soil Health	Maintains soil fertility	Builds and regenerates soil over time
Carbon Sequestration	Limited focus	Actively removes carbon from the atmosphere
Biodiversity	Preserves existing biodiversity	Actively increases plant and animal diversity
Water Management	Efficient use of water	Improves water retention and restores water cycles
Farming Approach	Still uses some modern inputs like fertilizers	Fully natural methods with no chemicals
Long-Term Impact	Prevents degradation	Improves land productivity over generations

While both approaches are better than conventional farming, **regenerative agriculture offers long-term benefits** that go beyond sustainability.

3.5 How Regenerative Agriculture Works in Practice

Regenerative farming **mimics natural ecosystems** to create self-sustaining agricultural systems. Here are some key techniques used in regenerative farming:

3.5.1 No-Till or Minimal-Till Farming

Problem: Conventional tilling disrupts soil structure, kills beneficial microbes, and increases erosion.
Solution: No-till farming preserves soil integrity, allowing natural organisms to enrich the soil.

3.5.2 Cover Cropping & Green Manure

Problem: Leaving soil bare leads to erosion, loss of nutrients, and weed growth.
Solution: Planting cover crops (like clover or legumes) keeps soil covered, adds organic matter, and fixes nitrogen naturally.

3.5.3 Agroforestry & Perennial Crops

Problem: Monoculture farming strips soil of nutrients and destroys biodiversity.
Solution: Growing trees alongside crops creates a diverse ecosystem that improves soil and provides additional income sources.

3.5.4 Rotational Grazing & Livestock Integration

Problem: Overgrazing depletes soil nutrients and leads to desertification.
Solution: Rotational grazing allows land to recover, increases soil organic matter, and improves pasture health.

3.5.5 Composting & Natural Fertilizers

Problem: Synthetic fertilizers degrade soil over time and contribute to pollution.
Solution: Using compost, manure, and microbial inoculants enhances soil fertility without synthetic inputs.

These methods **not only sustain farming but actively regenerate land**, making it more productive with each passing season.

3.6 The Role of Regenerative Agriculture in Climate Change Mitigation

Climate change is one of the biggest challenges facing global agriculture. Regenerative farming **helps reverse climate change** in three major ways:

1. **Carbon Sequestration** – Healthy soil absorbs and stores atmospheric carbon, reducing greenhouse gases.
2. **Drought and Flood Resilience** – Improved soil structure retains water, reducing the impact of extreme weather.
3. **Reducing Chemical Pollution** – Eliminating synthetic fertilizers and pesticides prevents contamination of soil and water.

Many studies show that regenerative farms **can act as carbon sinks**, helping to offset emissions from agriculture and industry.

3.7 Economic and Social Benefits of Regenerative Agriculture

Regenerative farming is not just good for the environment—it also offers **economic and social benefits** for farmers and communities.

3.7.1 Increased Profitability

☑ Lower input costs (no synthetic fertilizers or pesticides).
☑ Higher yields over time as soil fertility improves.
☑ Diversified income from agroforestry, livestock, and organic produce.

3.7.2 Improved Farmer Livelihoods

- Less reliance on expensive external inputs.
- More resilient farms that withstand extreme weather.
- Stronger rural communities through local food production.

3.7.3 Better Food Security & Nutrition

- Healthier, chemical-free food.
- More resilient food systems, reducing dependency on industrial agriculture.

By restoring the land, **regenerative farming supports farmers, consumers, and the planet alike.**

3.8 Conclusion: The Future is Regenerative

Sustainable agriculture is a good first step, but **regenerative agriculture is the future** of farming. By focusing on soil health, biodiversity, and climate resilience, regenerative farming offers a **pathway to a truly self-sustaining and productive agricultural system.**

Key Takeaways from This Chapter:

✓**Sustainable agriculture** aims to reduce harm, while **regenerative agriculture** actively restores ecosystems.
✓**Regenerative techniques** like no-till farming, agroforestry, and composting improve soil and water retention.
✓**Regenerative farming fights climate change** by storing carbon and making farms more resilient.
✓**Economically, regenerative farms** reduce input costs and provide stable long-term profits.

As more farmers adopt **regenerative practices**, we move closer to a world where food production **enhances nature rather than depleting it.**

Chapter 4: Soil Regeneration Without Chemicals

(Restoring Soil Health Through Natural and Sustainable Methods)

4.1 Introduction: Why Soil Regeneration is Crucial

Soil is the **foundation of all life on land**, it supports plant growth, maintains biodiversity, and plays a vital role in the water cycle. However, modern industrial farming has severely degraded soil worldwide. Decades of **chemical fertilizers, pesticides, monocropping, and excessive tilling** have left vast tracts of farmland infertile, compacted, and vulnerable to erosion.

To ensure food security and environmental health, farmers must focus on **regenerating soil without the use of synthetic chemicals**. This chapter explores the natural techniques used in **soil regeneration**, focusing on organic matter, microbial activity, and ecosystem balance.

4.2 The Problems with Chemical-Based Soil Management

Conventional farming relies heavily on synthetic fertilizers and pesticides to increase crop yields. While these methods provide short-term benefits, they create **long-term damage** to soil health.

4.2.1 How Chemical Farming Harms the Soil

1. **Loss of Soil Microbial Life** – Synthetic fertilizers disrupt the balance of beneficial bacteria and fungi, reducing natural nutrient cycling.
2. **Soil Acidification** – Overuse of chemical fertilizers, especially nitrogen-based ones, leads to acidic soils, making essential nutrients unavailable to plants.
3. **Nutrient Imbalance & Dependency** – Chemical fertilizers provide immediate nutrients, but they do not replenish organic matter, leading to long-term soil depletion.
4. **Compaction & Reduced Water Retention** – Tilling and chemical inputs degrade soil structure, making it harder for roots to penetrate and absorb water.
5. **Toxic Residues & Pollution** – Pesticides and synthetic inputs contaminate water sources, harming both ecosystems and human health.

By eliminating synthetic chemicals and **adopting regenerative methods**, farmers can rebuild soil fertility while improving productivity in the long run.

4.3 Principles of Soil Regeneration Without Chemicals

Restoring soil health requires **mimicking natural ecosystems**. Instead of relying on external inputs, natural farming encourages **soil-building processes** that occur in forests and grasslands.

The Key Principles of Soil Regeneration:

✓**Increase Organic Matter** – Compost, mulch, and cover crops enrich soil nutrients naturally.
✓**Promote Microbial Life** – Encouraging beneficial bacteria, fungi, and earthworms creates a self-sustaining soil ecosystem.
✓**Reduce Soil Disturbance** – No-till or minimum-till farming protects soil structure.
✓**Enhance Biodiversity** – Crop rotation, polyculture, and agroforestry prevent soil degradation.
✓**Improve Water Retention** – Techniques like mulching and deep-rooted crops help soil absorb and retain moisture.

By following these principles, farmers can **restore soil health without using a single drop of synthetic chemicals.**

4.4 Natural Methods for Soil Regeneration

There are several **tried-and-tested techniques** that regenerate soil naturally. These methods not only restore soil fertility but also make farms more **resilient to droughts, pests, and extreme weather conditions**.

4.4.1 Composting: Nature's Fertilizer

Compost is one of the **most effective ways** to regenerate soil. It provides nutrients, enhances microbial activity, and improves soil structure.

How Composting Works:

- **Organic waste** (food scraps, leaves, manure) decomposes naturally.
- **Microorganisms** break down the material, creating nutrient-rich humus.
- **Finished compost** is mixed into the soil to improve fertility.

Benefits of Composting:

- Improves **soil aeration** and **moisture retention**.
- Enhances **microbial activity**, reducing the need for synthetic fertilizers.
- Restores **nutrient balance** in depleted soils.

4.4.2 Mulching: A Protective Blanket for Soil

Mulching involves covering the soil with organic materials like **straw, leaves, or wood chips**.

Benefits of Mulching:

- Prevents **soil erosion** and **moisture loss**.
- Suppresses **weeds naturally**, reducing the need for herbicides.

- Feeds beneficial microbes as it slowly decomposes.

4.4.3 Cover Cropping: Regenerating Soil with Living Plants

Cover crops, such as **clover, alfalfa, and mustard**, help restore soil health by:

✓ Fixing **nitrogen** in the soil (leguminous plants like peas and beans).
✓ Preventing **erosion** by keeping the soil covered.
✓ Suppressing **weeds and pests** naturally.

Cover crops act as **green manure** when ploughed back into the soil, adding organic matter and improving fertility.

4.4.4 No-Till or Minimum-Till Farming

Tilling disturbs the **natural structure** of soil, leading to erosion and loss of microbial life. No-till farming preserves soil health by:

✓ Allowing **roots and microbes** to break down organic matter naturally.
✓ Enhancing **soil carbon sequestration**.
✓ Retaining more **water**, reducing irrigation needs.

4.4.5 Vermiculture: Using Earthworms to Improve Soil

Earthworms play a **crucial role** in soil regeneration by:

- Breaking down **organic matter** into nutrient-rich castings.
- Aerating soil, improving **water infiltration**.
- Enhancing **microbial life** and overall soil health.

By using **vermicomposting**, farmers can produce **nutrient-rich organic fertilizer** that improves soil fertility.

Vermicompost

4.5 Restoring Soil Fertility Through Microbial Solutions

Healthy soil depends on a thriving microbial ecosystem. Several natural bio-enhancers can help restore microbial balance:

4.5.1 Jeevamrit and Beejamrit (Indian Traditional Soil Boosters)

Developed by **Subhash Palekar's Zero Budget Natural Farming (ZBNF)**, these solutions boost soil microbes.

Jeevamrit (Microbial Tonic for Soil)
Ingredients:

- Cow dung and urine (from indigenous cows)
- Jaggery, pulse flour, and soil from a healthy field
- Water (fermented for 2-3 days)

Benefits:

- Enhances soil microbes and nutrient cycling.
- Increases plant immunity against pests and diseases.

Beejamrit (Seed Treatment Solution)

- Used to coat seeds before planting, **protecting against pathogens** and improving germination rates.

4.5.2 Biochar: Charcoal for Soil Health

Biochar is **carbon-rich charcoal** that improves soil structure and microbial activity.

Benefits of Biochar:

- Retains **moisture and nutrients** for long periods.
- Increases **soil carbon sequestration**, reducing CO_2 emissions.
- Enhances microbial activity, reducing the need for fertilizers.

4.5.3 Indigenous Microorganism (IMO) Solutions

IMO-based solutions, often used in **Korean Natural Farming**, involve collecting local microbes from forest soil and fermenting them to create a powerful soil booster.

Benefits of IMOs:

- Strengthen soil's **natural microbiome**.
- Improve **nutrient absorption** in plants.
- Reduce **dependency on external inputs**.

4.6 The Long-Term Benefits of Chemical-Free Soil Regeneration

Shifting away from chemicals to **natural soil regeneration techniques** provides multiple benefits:

Environmental Impact:
✓ Reduces **pollution** of water bodies and air.
✓ Enhances **carbon sequestration**, mitigating climate change.

Farmer Benefits:
✓ Lower input costs (no expensive fertilizers or pesticides).
✓ Increased soil productivity over time.

Healthier Food:
✓ Produces **chemical-free, nutrient-rich** crops.
✓ Reduces exposure to toxic residues in food.

4.7 Conclusion: Regenerating Soil for Future Generations

By **eliminating chemicals** and adopting **natural soil regeneration techniques**, farmers can restore degraded lands, improve food security, and **create a more resilient farming system**.

Key Takeaways:
✓ Compost, mulch, and cover crops build healthy soil.
✓ No-till and vermiculture enhance microbial activity.
✓Jeevamrit, biochar, and IMOs restore soil fertility naturally.

Soil is **alive**—and with the right methods, we can **heal and sustain it for generations to come.**

Chapter 5: Zero Budget Natural Farming (ZBNF)
(A Revolutionary Approach to Farming Without External Costs)

5.1 Introduction: The Need for Zero Budget Natural Farming

In many parts of the world, farmers are trapped in a vicious cycle of debt. The high costs of seeds, synthetic fertilizers, pesticides, and irrigation push small farmers into financial distress. In India, for example, thousands of farmers have struggled with mounting debts due to increasing input costs.

To solve this crisis, **Subhash Palekar**, an Indian agricultural scientist and farmer, developed **Zero Budget Natural Farming (ZBNF)**—a method that allows farmers to cultivate crops **without spending money on external inputs like fertilizers and pesticides**. ZBNF is a sustainable, chemical-free farming practice that promotes soil health, biodiversity, and self-sufficiency.

This chapter explores the **principles, methods, and benefits of ZBNF**, showing how farmers can grow crops naturally while reducing costs to zero.

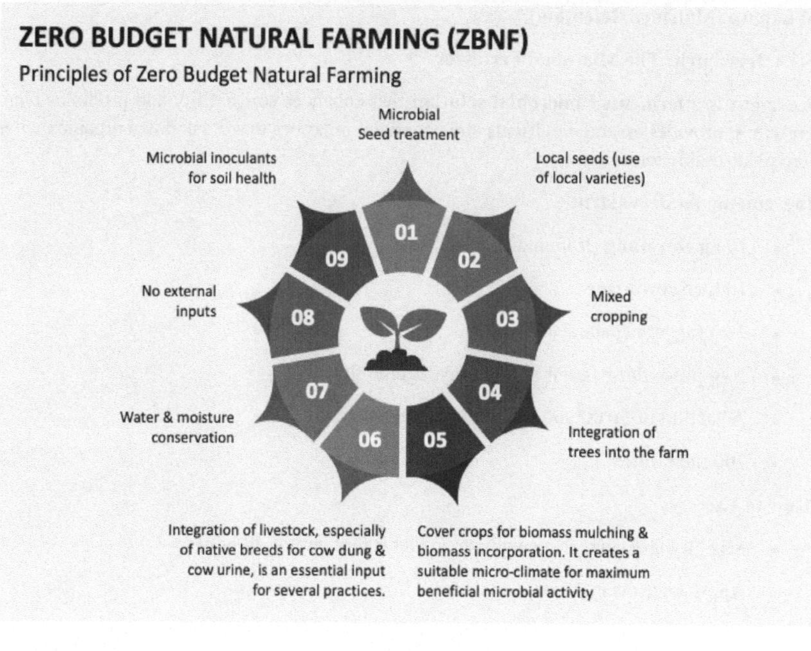

5.2 What is Zero Budget Natural Farming?

ZBNF is based on **working with nature instead of against it**. The system uses natural, locally available resources to fertilize soil, protect crops, and enhance biodiversity.

Key Features of ZBNF:

1. **No Synthetic Chemicals** – No artificial fertilizers, pesticides, or genetically modified seeds.
2. **Self-Sufficiency** – Farmers use their own cow dung, urine, and natural resources to produce fertilizers and pesticides.
3. **Soil Health Improvement** – Encourages soil microbial life and organic matter.
4. **Cost-Free Farming** – Reduces input costs to near zero, making farming more profitable.
5. **Water Conservation** – Uses techniques like mulching to retain moisture and reduce irrigation needs.

Unlike organic farming, which still requires **external inputs like bio-fertilizers and compost**, ZBNF **eliminates the need for any outside products**.

5.3 The Four Pillars of ZBNF

Subhash Palekar developed four key formulations that serve as the foundation of Zero Budget Natural Farming. These include **Jeevamrit, Beejamrit, Acchadana (Mulching), and Whapasa (Moisture Retention).**

5.3.1 Jeevamrit: The Microbial Fertilizer

Jeevamrit is a **fermented microbial solution** that enhances soil fertility and promotes plant growth. It provides essential nutrients and beneficial microbes that break down organic matter into plant-usable forms.

Ingredients for Jeevamrit:

- 10 kg **cow dung** (from indigenous cows)
- 10 liters**cow urine**
- 2 kg **jaggery** (natural sugar)
- 2 kg **pulse flour** (gram flour or any legume flour)
- A handful of **forest soil** (rich in microorganisms)
- 200 liters**water**

How to Use:

- Mix all ingredients in a container and let it ferment for **48 hours**.
- Apply **once every 15 days** to the soil.

Ghanajeevamrit

Benefits of Jeevamrit:

✔ Supplies essential **nutrients and microbes** to the soil.
✔ Converts non-available nutrients into **plant-available** forms.
✔ Eliminates the need for **chemical fertilizers**.

5.3.2 Beejamrit: The Seed Treatment Solution

Beejamrit is a **natural seed treatment** that protects young plants from pests and diseases. It enhances germination rates and ensures strong, disease-resistant crops.

Beejamrit

Ingredients for Beejamrit:

- 5 kg **cow dung**
- 5 liters**cow urine**
- 1 liter**lime water**
- A handful of **soil from a healthy field**
- 20 liters**water**

How to Use:

- Dip seeds in the solution for **30 minutes** before planting.

Benefits of Beejamrit:

✓ Prevents **fungal and bacterial infections** in seedlings.

✓ Improves **germination rates** and seedling strength.

✓ Protects plants without using **chemical fungicides**.

5.3.3 Acchadana: Mulching for Soil Protection

Mulching (Acchadana) involves covering the soil with **organic materials** like dry leaves, straw, or green manure. This technique **mimics nature**, keeping the soil moist and nutrient-rich.

Mulching in Mustard field

Types of Mulching:

- **Straw Mulching** – Dry plant matter covers the soil, reducing evaporation.
- **Green Mulching** – Living plants (cover crops) protect the soil and add nutrients.
- **Soil Mulching** – A layer of compost or manure to improve soil fertility.

Benefits of Mulching:

✓ Prevents **soil erosion** and **water loss.**

✓ Increases **earthworm activity** and microbial life.

✓ Suppresses **weed growth** naturally.

5.3.4 Whapasa: Moisture Retention for Water Conservation

Whapasa is the **concept of maintaining soil moisture** through microbial activity and organic matter rather than excessive irrigation.

Principles of Whapasa:

- Instead of **over-irrigating**, maintain a balance of air and moisture in the soil.
- Apply **Jeevamrit and mulch** to improve **water retention**.
- Avoid deep plowing to **preserve soil moisture**.

Benefits of Whapasa:
✓ Reduces **water consumption** by up to 60%.
✓ Improves **drought resistance** in crops.
✓ Prevents **waterlogging** and root diseases.

5.4 Benefits of ZBNF for Farmers and the Environment

ZBNF is gaining popularity worldwide because of its **economic, environmental, and social benefits.**

5.4.1 Economic Benefits

Cost Savings – Farmers eliminate the need for synthetic fertilizers and pesticides.
Higher Profits – Lower costs mean more income per harvest.
Financial Security – Reduces dependency on loans and debts.

5.4.2 Environmental Benefits

Soil Restoration – Builds organic matter and microbial life.
Water Conservation – Reduces irrigation needs and prevents runoff.
Climate Resilience – Increases carbon sequestration and soil fertility.

5.4.3 Social Benefits

Empowers Small Farmers – Reduces financial risks and dependency on corporations.
Healthier Food – No chemical residues, making food safer to eat.
Community Farming – Encourages knowledge sharing and collective farming efforts.

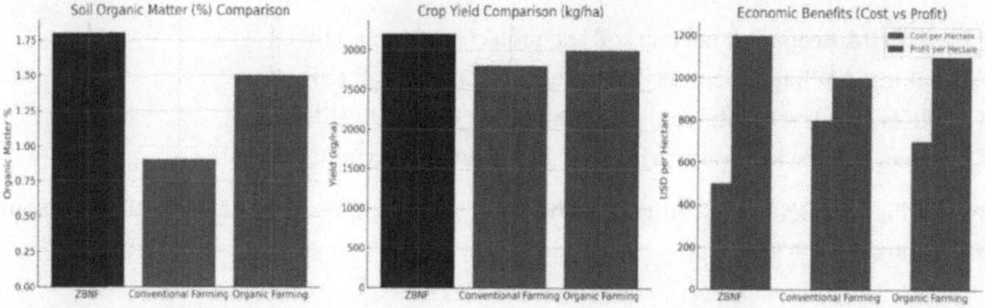

5.5 Success Stories of ZBNF Farmers

Many farmers across India and other countries have successfully adopted **ZBNF** with **impressive results.**

- **Andhra Pradesh, India**: The government is implementing ZBNF across 6 million farms, reducing chemical dependency.
- **Karnataka, India**: A farmer named Bhaskar Save increased yields while completely eliminating external inputs.

- **Maharashtra, India**: Mango and pomegranate farmers report better fruit quality and disease resistance.

These success stories prove that **ZBNF is not just an alternative—it is the future of farming**.

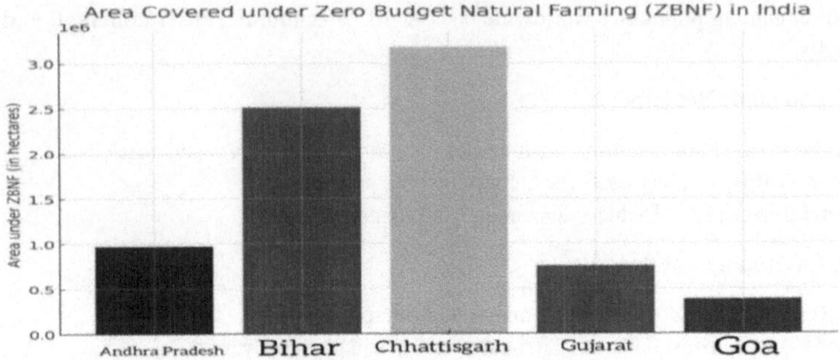

5.6 Conclusion: The Future of Farming is Zero Budget

Zero Budget Natural Farming **empowers farmers, protects the environment**, and **produces healthier food**. By using **indigenous knowledge and natural resources**, farmers can achieve food security **without financial burden**.

Key Takeaways from This Chapter:

✓**Jeevamrit&Beejamrit** nourish soil and protect seeds naturally.

✓**Mulching &Whapasa** conserve moisture and prevent soil erosion.

✓**ZBNF is cost-free, sustainable, and improves farmer livelihoods.**

✓**Farmers worldwide are proving that Zero Budget Farming works!**

By shifting to **ZBNF, agriculture can be truly sustainable—without debt, chemicals, or environmental harm.**

Chapter 6: Companion Planting & Polyculture

(Harnessing Plant Diversity for a Resilient and Productive Farm)

6.1 Introduction: The Power of Plant Diversity

For centuries, traditional farmers have relied on **companion planting and polyculture** to enhance soil fertility, prevent pests, and maximize harvests. Unlike modern monoculture farmingwhich grows a single crop over large areas; **polyculture integrates multiple crops together**, creating a balanced ecosystem that mimics nature.

Companion planting and polyculture offer a natural way to:

- ✓ Improve **soil health** and **increase biodiversity**.
- ✓ Reduce **pests and diseases** without chemicals.
- ✓ Enhance **crop yields** by optimizing space and nutrients.

In this chapter, we explore **the science behind plant partnerships, best companion plant combinations, and the benefits of multi-crop farming**.

6.2 What is Companion Planting?

Companion planting is the practice of **growing specific plants together** to enhance growth, deter pests, and improve soil health. Certain plants have natural chemical properties that benefit their neighbors, creating **synergistic relationships** that improve overall farm productivity.

Examples of Companion Planting:

- **Corn + Beans + Squash** (The "Three Sisters" Method)
- **Basil + Tomatoes** (Improves flavor and repels pests)
- **Sunflowers + Cucumbers** (Provides shade and support for vines)

6.3 Benefits of Companion Planting

6.3.1 Natural Pest Control

Some plants release natural compounds that repel pests or attract beneficial insects.

- **Marigolds** deter nematodes and aphids.
- **Garlic and Onions** repel common vegetable pests.
- **Basil** repels mosquitoes and enhances the growth of tomatoes.

6.3.2 Improved Soil Health

- **Legumes** (like beans and peas) **fix nitrogen** in the soil, reducing the need for fertilizers.
- **Deep-rooted plants** (like radishes) **break up compacted soil**, improving aeration.
- **Mulch-producing plants** (like clover) **reduce evaporation and suppress weeds.**

6.3.3 Efficient Space Utilization

Companion planting allows farmers to **grow more food in less space** by using vertical and horizontal growing patterns.

- **Tall plants (corn)** provide shade and support for **climbing plants (beans).**
- **Low-growing plants (lettuce)** provide ground cover that **retains soil moisture.**

6.3.4 Enhanced Crop Flavor& Growth

Certain plants improve the **taste and nutritional value** of their neighbors.

- **Basil enhances the flavor of tomatoes.**
- **Chamomile improves the taste of onions and cabbages.**

6.4 Best Companion Planting Combinations

Crop	Best Companions	Avoid Planting With
Tomatoes	Basil, onions, carrots, marigolds	Cabbage, potatoes, corn
Carrots	Onions, leeks, rosemary, beans	Dill
Corn	Beans, squash, sunflowers	Tomatoes
Lettuce	Radish, carrots, strawberries	Cabbage
Cabbage	Dill, celery, onions, chamomile	Strawberries, tomatoes

Companion planting **mimics natural ecosystems** by grouping plants that **support each other**, reducing the need for chemical inputs.

6.5 What is Polyculture?

Polyculture is the practice of **growing multiple crops in the same space** instead of relying on monoculture (single-crop farming). It is **one of the most effective ways to regenerate soil, prevent pests, and increase farm biodiversity**.

6.5.1 Types of Polyculture

i. **Row Polyculture** – Different crops are planted in alternating rows.
ii. **Intercropping** – Two or more crops are grown together in the same area.
iii. **Agroforestry** – Trees, shrubs, and crops are planted together.
iv. **Permaculture Systems** – A mix of vegetables, fruits, herbs, and animals in a self-sustaining ecosystem.

Intercropping lentil in mustard field

6.6 Benefits of Polyculture Farming

6.6.1 Increased Biodiversity

Monoculture depletes soil nutrients and attracts pests, while polyculture encourages **diverse plant and animal life**, reducing the need for pesticides.

6.6.2 Pest and Disease Reduction

Polyculture naturally **disrupts pest cycles**. When multiple crops are grown together, pests cannot easily find their target crops.

6.6.3 Soil Fertility Improvement

- **Legumes (beans, peas, clover)** fix nitrogen.
- **Deep-rooted crops (alfalfa, carrots)** bring up minerals from deep soil layers.
- **Leafy crops (lettuce, spinach)** add organic matter to the topsoil.

6.6.4 Greater Yield Per Acre

By combining plants with **different growth habits**, farmers can produce **more food in the same space**.

Example: In a **corn + beans + squash** polyculture system:

- Corn provides vertical support.
- Beans fix nitrogen for soil fertility.
- Squash spreads across the ground, preventing weed growth.

6.7 How to Implement Companion Planting & Polyculture on Your Farm

6.7.1 Step 1: Plan Crop Groupings

- Identify plants that **complement each other**.
- Avoid planting crops that **compete for the same nutrients.**

6.7.2 Step 2: Use Different Growth Heights

- Grow **tall plants (corn, sunflowers)** alongside **low-growing plants (lettuce, squash)**.

6.7.3 Step 3: Rotate Crops Each Season

- Change crop placements annually to **prevent soil depletion** and **control pests.**

6.7.4 Step 4: Include Flowers and Herbs

- Plant **marigolds, lavender, and chamomile** to attract pollinators and deter pests.

6.7.5 Step 5: Integrate Animals (Optional)

- Chickens help control insects.
- Cows and goats **fertilize the soil** naturally.

By following these **simple steps**, farmers can create a **self-sustaining ecosystem** that produces **healthy, chemical-free crops.**

6.8 Companion Planting & Polyculture Success Stories

Many farmers worldwide have **abandoned monoculture in favor of polyculture**, leading to **higher yields and healthier soil.**

Case Study 1:

The "Three Sisters" Method (North America)
Indigenous farmers in North America developed a **legendary companion planting system** using **corn, beans, and squash**. This system:
✓**Improves soil fertility** (beans fix nitrogen).
✓**Maximizes space** (corn provides climbing support).
✓**Reduces weeds** (squash shades the ground).

Case Study 2 :

Rice-Duck Farming (Japan & Philippines)
Farmers introduced **ducks into rice paddies**, leading to:
✓**Weed and pest control** (ducks eat pests).
✓**Natural fertilization** (duck manure improves soil).
✓**Higher rice yields** with **zero chemicals.**

These success stories show that **nature-based farming methods are more productive and sustainable** than monoculture.

6.9 Conclusion: The Future is Polyculture

Monoculture farming has caused **soil degradation, pest outbreaks, and nutrient depletion.** The solution? **Companion planting and polyculture.**

Key Takeaways:

✓ Companion planting **improves soil, repels pests, and increases yields.**

✓ Polyculture farming **mimics natural ecosystems, reducing the need for chemicals.**

✓ Smart plant pairings **boost flavor, nutrition, and plant health.**

✓ Integrating **animals, flowers, and herbs** creates a **balanced farm ecosystem.**

By embracing **plant diversity**, farmers can build **a healthier, more productive, and more sustainable future.**

Chapter 7: Water Conservation and Management

(Sustainable Strategies for Efficient Water Use in Natural Farming)

7.1 Introduction: The Importance of Water in Agriculture

Water is **the lifeblood of farming**. Every plant needs water to grow, transport nutrients, and produce food. However, **water scarcity** is becoming a major global crisis. Climate change, deforestation, and unsustainable farming practices have led to **droughts, depleted groundwater, and inefficient irrigation**.

To ensure **long-term farm productivity**, farmers must adopt **sustainable water conservation and management techniques**. **Natural farming** focuses on using water **wisely**, reducing dependency on irrigation, and restoring the **natural water cycle**.

This chapter explores **water-efficient farming techniques, rainwater harvesting, soil moisture retention, and irrigation innovations** to help farmers use water **sustainably and effectively**.

7.2 The Problems with Conventional Water Use in Farming

Most modern farms rely heavily on **groundwater and surface water sources**, leading to:

Overuse of Groundwater – Excessive pumping lowers water tables, drying up wells.
Inefficient Irrigation – Flood irrigation wastes more water than it delivers.
Soil Degradation – Excessive watering can **wash away nutrients**, leading to **salinity and erosion**.
Climate Change Effects – Droughts and irregular rainfall patterns make water availability unpredictable.

To combat these challenges, **natural water conservation methods** focus on **storing, reusing, and maximizing water efficiency**.

7.3 Key Principles of Water Conservation in Natural Farming

To maintain a **self-sufficient water system**, natural farmers follow these core principles:

✓**Minimize water loss** through evaporation and runoff.
✓**Improve soil moisture retention** using organic methods.
✓**Harvest and store rainwater** for future use.
✓**Use water-efficient irrigation systems** to avoid wastage.
✓**Work with natural landscapes** to restore local water cycles.

By implementing **these strategies**, farms can remain productive even in dry conditions.

7.4 Natural Farming Techniques for Water Conservation

7.4.1 Mulching: A Natural Way to Retain Soil Moisture

Mulching involves covering the soil with **organic materials** like straw, dry leaves, or wood chips. This **reduces evaporation, keeps the soil cool, and prevents erosion**.

Benefits of Mulching:

- ✓ Retains **moisture**, reducing the need for irrigation.
- ✓ Prevents **weed growth**, which competes for water.
- ✓ Encourages **earthworms and microbes**, improving soil structure.

Example: Farmers using straw mulch in dry regions **reduce water use by 50%** while increasing crop yields.

7.4.2 Whapasa: The Indian Concept of Moisture Balance

Developed by **Subhash Palekar**, Whapasa refers to **maintaining soil moisture without over-irrigation**.

How Whapasa Works:

- Instead of **overwatering**, farmers irrigate **only when necessary**.
- Applying **Jeevamrit** and mulch helps **microbes retain moisture** in the soil.
- Reducing **plowing and tillage** prevents water loss from the topsoil.

Benefits of Whapasa:

✓ Prevents **waterlogging** and **root rot**.
✓ Reduces **water use by up to 60%**.
✓ Keeps soil **moist but not saturated**, improving plant health.

7.4.3 Cover Cropping: A Living Water Sponge

Cover crops are **non-harvested plants** (such as clover, mustard, and legumes) grown to **protect and enrich the soil**.

How Cover Crops Help Water Conservation:

- Reduce **water runoff** by absorbing excess rainwater.
- Increase **soil organic matter**, improving moisture retention.
- Act as **natural mulch**, reducing evaporation.

Example: In drought-prone areas, farmers plant **leguminous cover crops** to **trap moisture and fix nitrogen**, reducing the need for irrigation and fertilizers.

7.4.4 Agroforestry: Trees for Water Conservation

Integrating trees into farms **improves water retention and prevents soil drying**.

How Trees Help:

- ✓ **Deep roots** pull up groundwater for crops.
- ✓ **Shade reduces evaporation**, keeping soil moist.
- ✓ **Leaves add organic matter**, improving soil water-holding capacity.

Example: In arid parts of Africa, farmers plant **acacia trees** alongside crops to **increase water availability** and **prevent desertification.**

7.5 Rainwater Harvesting: Storing Nature's Gift

Rainwater is a **free** and **sustainable** water source. Capturing and storing rainwater helps farmers reduce **dependency on groundwater and irrigation systems.**

7.5.1 Methods of Rainwater Harvesting

- **Rooftop Collection:** Directing rainwater from roofs into storage tanks.
- **Farm Ponds:** Small water reservoirs that store rainwater for later use.
- **Swales and Trenches:** Shallow ditches along slopes that **slow down water runoff**, allowing it to **soak into the soil.**
- **Check Dams & Percolation Pits:** Structures that help **recharge groundwater levels.**

Benefits of Rainwater Harvesting:

✓ Provides **free water** for irrigation.

✓ Replenishes **groundwater tables.**

✓ Reduces **soil erosion and flooding.**

Example: Farmers in Rajasthan, India, use **traditional rainwater storage tanks** (called **Johads**) to **restore groundwater levels**, reviving farmland in dry regions.

7.6 Efficient Irrigation Systems for Water Conservation

Traditional irrigation methods, like **flood irrigation**, waste more water than they deliver. Instead, natural farmers use **efficient irrigation systems** that reduce water loss.

7.6.1 Drip Irrigation: Delivering Water Directly to the Roots

Drip irrigation uses **small pipes with tiny holes** to release water **drop by drop** directly at the plant's roots.

Advantages of Drip Irrigation:

✓**Saves 60-80% of water** compared to flood irrigation.

✓ Reduces **weed growth** (since only crops receive water).

✓ Improves **nutrient absorption.**

Example: In Israel, farmers use **drip irrigation** to **grow crops in the desert**, achieving high yields with minimal water.

7.6.2 Clay Pot Irrigation: A Low-Cost, Ancient Technique

Clay pot irrigation is a **traditional method** where **porous clay pots** are buried near crops and filled with water. The pots **slowly release moisture into the soil**, providing **steady hydration**.

Benefits of Clay Pot Irrigation:

✓**Uses 70% less water** than surface irrigation.

✓ Keeps soil **moist without overwatering.**

✓ Perfect for **small farms and home gardens.**

Example: Farmers in Mexico and Africa use **clay pot irrigation** in arid regions to **grow vegetables without external irrigation.**

7.7 Case Studies: Farmers Successfully Managing Water Sustainably

Case Study 1:
Rajendra Singh, "The Waterman of India"
Rajendra Singh revived **7 rivers and over 1,200 villages** in Rajasthan using **traditional rainwater harvesting techniques**. His efforts have **restored farmlands** in one of India's driest regions.

Case Study 2:
The Loess Plateau, China
Once a barren desert, the **Loess Plateau** was revived through **terracing, agroforestry, and rainwater harvesting**. The region **now supports agriculture and livestock**, proving that **degraded land can be restored** with the right techniques.

7.8 Conclusion: The Future of Water in Farming

Water is **the most precious resource in agriculture**. By adopting **water conservation techniques**, farmers can **protect water sources, increase yields, and withstand droughts**.

Key Takeaways:

✓**Mulching, Whapasa, and cover cropping** help retain soil moisture.

✓**Rainwater harvesting and swales** restore groundwater.

✓**Drip irrigation and clay pot irrigation** reduce water wastage.

✓**Agroforestry and polyculture** improve farm resilience.

By working **with nature, not against it**, farmers can secure a **sustainable and water-efficient future**.

Chapter 8: Pest and Disease Control Without Chemicals

(Harnessing Natural Methods for Healthy Crops and a Balanced Ecosystem)

8.1 Introduction: The Problem with Chemical-Based Pest Control

Pests and diseases are among the biggest challenges in farming, often causing significant crop losses. Conventional agriculture relies heavily on **chemical pesticides and fungicides**, which may offer quick solutions but create long-term problems:

Soil and Water Contamination – Pesticides seep into groundwater, polluting water sources.
Harm to Pollinators and Beneficial Insects – Chemical sprays kill not only pests but also bees, butterflies, and natural predators like ladybugs.
Pest Resistance – Over time, pests evolve resistance to synthetic chemicals, requiring even stronger pesticides.
Health Risks – Pesticide residues on food are linked to cancer, neurological disorders, and hormonal imbalances.

Natural farming **avoids synthetic chemicals**, instead using **biological, ecological, and plant-based solutions** to control pests and diseases. This chapter explores **natural pest management strategies** that maintain a healthy farm ecosystem while ensuring abundant harvests.

8.2 Principles of Natural Pest and Disease Control

Natural pest management focuses on **prevention rather than elimination**. Instead of killing pests with chemicals, farmers **strengthen plant immunity, attract beneficial insects, and use natural repellents**.

Key Principles:

✓**Healthy Soil = Healthy Plants** – Nutrient-rich soil strengthens plant immunity.
✓**Encourage Biodiversity** – Companion planting and polyculture naturally deter pests.
✓**Attract Natural Predators** – Birds, insects, and frogs help control pests.
✓**Use Plant-Based Pesticides** – Neem, garlic, and chili sprays repel insects.
✓**Crop Rotation & Trap Crops** – Break pest life cycles with smart planting.

By **working with nature**, farmers can control pests **without harming the environment or human health**.

8.3 Strengthening Plant Immunity to Prevent Pests and Diseases

Healthy plants **resist pests and diseases naturally**. The first step in pest control is **boosting plant immunity** through:

Jeevamrit and Beejamrit – These organic soil amendments (discussed in Chapter 5) supply microbes and nutrients that **increase plant resistance to infections**.
Composting and Mulching – Adding organic matter **improves soil structure** and enhances plant growth.
Using Indigenous Seeds – Local seed varieties are **naturally adapted** to resist regional pests and diseases.

When plants are strong and well-nourished, they **produce natural defense chemicals** that deter insects and infections.

8.4 Companion Planting for Pest Control

Certain plants **repel pests or attract beneficial insects** when grown together.

Best Companion Plant Combinations for Pest Control:

Crop	Companion Plants (Pest Repellents)	Pests Repelled
Tomatoes	Basil, marigold, garlic	Aphids, whiteflies
Cabbage	Thyme, rosemary, onions	Cabbage worms
Carrots	Chives, leeks	Carrot flies
Beans	Marigolds, nasturtiums	Bean beetles
Cucumbers	Sunflowers, radishes	Cucumber beetles

Example: Growing **marigolds** near vegetables repels nematodes and aphids while attracting pollinators.

8.5 Beneficial Insects: Nature's Pest Controllers

Instead of using chemical pesticides, **encourage beneficial insects** that **prey on pests**.

Ladybugs – Eat aphids, scale insects, and whiteflies.
Praying Mantises – Feed on grasshoppers, beetles, and moths.
Spiders – Capture flying insects like mosquitoes and flies.
Birds (e.g., Swallows & Sparrows) – Eat caterpillars, locusts, and grasshoppers.

How to Attract Beneficial Insects:

- ✓ Plant **flowering herbs** like fennel, dill, and cilantro.
- ✓ Provide **habitats** like hedgerows and nesting areas.
- ✓ Avoid chemical pesticides that kill helpful insects.

Example: Farmers in Africa use **flower strips** around crops to attract predators that **reduce aphid infestations by 80%**.

8.6 Homemade Organic Pest Repellents

Farmers can make **natural, non-toxic pesticides** using locally available ingredients.

8.6.1 Neem Oil Spray (Insect Repellent)

Neem oil is a powerful **antifungal and insect repellent**.

Ingredients:

- 50ml neem oil
- 1 liter water
- 5ml liquid soap (for emulsification)

How to Use:

- Mix well and spray on crops **once a week.**

Effective Against: Aphids, caterpillars, whiteflies, and fungal diseases.

8.6.2 Garlic-Chili Spray (Pest Deterrent)

Garlic and chili act as natural insect **repellents**.

Ingredients:

- 5 garlic cloves
- 5 chili peppers
- 1 liter water

How to Use:

- Blend ingredients, strain, and spray on plants.

Effective Against: Moths, caterpillars, and aphids.

8.6.3 Cow Urine Tonic (Antifungal & Pest Control)

Cow urine contains **antibacterial properties** that control plant diseases.

How to Use:

- **Dilute 1 part cow urine** with **10 parts water** and spray weekly.

Effective Against: Powdery mildew, bacterial wilt, and sucking insects.

Example: Indian farmers using **cow urine sprays** reported **50% fewer fungal infections** in crops.

8.7 Trap Crops: Diverting Pests Away from Main Crops

Trap cropping involves **growing specific plants that attract pests**, keeping them away from main crops.

Sunflowers – Attract aphids away from vegetables.
Mustard – Draws pests like flea beetles away from cabbage.
Nasturtiums – Lure aphids and whiteflies away from tomatoes.

Example: Rice farmers in Asia use **duckweed and water plants** as **pest-attracting crops**, reducing insect damage to rice paddies.

8.8 Crop Rotation: Breaking Pest and Disease Cycles

Growing the **same crop in the same place every year** attracts pests that specialize in that plant. **Crop rotation prevents this problem.**

Rotation Plan Example:
Year 1: Grow legumes (beans, peas) to fix nitrogen.
Year 2: Grow root vegetables (carrots, onions) to aerate soil.
Year 3: Grow leafy greens (lettuce, cabbage) for organic matter.
Year 4: Grow cereals (wheat, corn) for grain production.

Each year, pests **lose their food source**, reducing their population naturally.

8.9 Case Studies: Farmers Using Natural Pest Control

Case Study 1: Sikkim, India – 100% Organic Farming State

- Sikkim banned **chemical pesticides**, shifting entirely to **natural pest control methods** like neem oil, cow urine sprays, and companion planting.
- Results: **Higher soil fertility, improved biodiversity, and increased farmer profits.**

Case Study 2: Kenyan Farmers Using Push-Pull Pest Control

- **Push plants (desmodium)** repel maize pests, while **pull plants (napier grass)** attract them away.
- Results: **80% fewer pest infestations and increased corn yield.**

8.10 Conclusion: A Chemical-Free Future for Pest Control

Natural farming **proves that pesticides are unnecessary**. By using **biodiversity, plant-based repellents, and ecosystem balance**, farmers can control pests **without harming the environment or human health**.

Key Takeaways:

✓ Companion planting **repels pests naturally**.
✓ Beneficial insects **act as natural predators.**
✓ Neem, garlic, and chili sprays **replace chemical pesticides.**
✓ Crop rotation and trap crops **break pest cycles.**

With these **sustainable methods**, farmers can **protect their crops naturally** while ensuring a **healthy, chemical-free harvest.**

Chapter 9: Transitioning from Conventional to Natural Farming

(A Step-by-Step Guide to Adopting Sustainable and Chemical-Free Agriculture)

9.1 Introduction: Why Transition to Natural Farming?

For decades, industrial agriculture has relied on **chemical fertilizers, pesticides, and heavy machinery** to maximize yields. While these methods provide short-term gains, they **deplete soil health, increase costs, and contribute to environmental degradation**.

Transitioning to **natural farming** offers a sustainable alternative. By restoring soil fertility, **reducing input costs, and working with nature**, farmers can achieve **higher long-term productivity and financial stability**.

Common Fears About Transitioning:
Will my yields drop? → Yields may initially decline but **improve as soil health restores**.

Is natural farming profitable? → Yes! Costs decrease significantly as **farmers stop buying fertilizers and pesticides**.

Does it require more labor? → Initially, yes, but over time, **natural systems reduce labor needs**.

This chapter provides a **practical roadmap** for farmers looking to shift from conventional farming to **sustainable, chemical-free agriculture**.

9.2 Understanding the Challenges of Transition

Transitioning from conventional to natural farming is not just about **stopping chemical use**—it requires **changing the entire farming system**.

9.2.1 Initial Challenges Faced by Farmers

- ✓ **Soil Fertility Decline** – The soil is initially **dependent on chemical inputs**. It takes time for microbes to rebuild fertility.
- ✓ **Pest and Disease Management** – Without pesticides, **initial pest outbreaks may occur**. Companion planting and natural repellents help.
- ✓ **Water Management Shifts** – Moving away from conventional irrigation requires **improved soil moisture retention techniques**.
- ✓ **Yield Fluctuations** – The first 1-2 years may show **lower yields** until the ecosystem stabilizes.

Solution: Understanding these challenges **before transitioning** helps farmers **prepare strategies to overcome them**.

9.3 The Three-Phase Transition Plan

Transitioning can be done **gradually** in three phases to ensure success.

Phase 1: Soil Preparation (First Year)

- **Stop Chemical Fertilizers Gradually**: Reduce synthetic inputs **by 25-50%** while increasing organic amendments.
- **Start Composting**: Prepare and apply **Jeevamrit, Beejamrit, and Vermicompost**.
- **Use Cover Crops**: Plant legumes (clover, beans) to **fix nitrogen** naturally.
- **Introduce Mulching**: Apply straw, leaves, or green manure to **retain moisture and suppress weeds**.

Example: Farmers in Maharashtra, India, gradually reduced **chemical fertilizers** while adding Jeevamrit, leading to **higher organic matter** in their soil within a year.

Phase 2: Pest and Disease Control (Second Year)

- **Stop Synthetic Pesticides**: Replace with **Neem, Garlic-Chili Spray, and Cow Urine Mix**.
- **Introduce Beneficial Insects**: Attract ladybugs, praying mantises, and birds.
- **Practice Companion Planting**: Pair crops like **tomatoes with basil, or cabbage with thyme** to repel pests naturally.
- **Start Crop Rotation**: Prevent soil depletion and pest build-up by alternating crops.

Example: A farmer in Kenya used **push-pull pest control** (desmodium repelling pests,napier grass attracting them), reducing **maize pest infestations by 80%**.

Phase 3: Ecosystem Restoration & Full Transition (Third Year & Beyond)

- **Fully eliminate synthetic inputs** and let nature take over.
- **Enhance Biodiversity** by integrating **agroforestry, livestock, and mixed cropping**.
- **Improve Water Efficiency** with **rainwater harvesting and soil moisture retention**.
- **Diversify Income Sources** by adding **horticulture, beekeeping, or medicinal plants**.

Example: Farmers in Andhra Pradesh, India, completely transitioned to **Zero Budget Natural Farming (ZBNF)**, eliminating input costs while **improving soil quality and profits**.

9.4 Practical Techniques to Support a Smooth Transition

9.4.1 Composting and Natural Fertilizers

Switching from chemical fertilizers to **natural soil amendments** is critical.

Best Organic Fertilizers for Transitioning Farms:

- **Jeevamrit (Liquid Microbial Fertilizer)** – Boosts soil microbes.
- **Vermicompost (Earthworm-Based Compost)** – Enriches soil nutrients.
- **Biochar (Carbon-Rich Charcoal)** – Improves water retention.
- **Green Manure (Cover Crops)** – Fixes nitrogen naturally.

Example: Farmers in Nepal **increased wheat yields by 30%** after replacing synthetic fertilizers with vermicompost.

9.4.2 Natural Pest and Disease Control

Instead of synthetic pesticides, use **biological and plant-based repellents**.

Best Natural Pest Management Techniques:

- **Neem Oil Spray** – Controls aphids, whiteflies, and fungi.
- **Marigolds & Basil** – Repel nematodes and mosquitoes.
- **Trap Cropping (e.g., Mustard with Cabbage)** – Lures pests away from main crops.
- **Beneficial Insects (Ladybugs, Spiders, Frogs)** – Eat harmful pests.

Example: Farmers in Indonesia replaced pesticides with **Neem Spray + Companion Planting**, reducing **pest damage by 70%.**

9.4.3 Water Management & Rainwater Harvesting

Water conservation becomes more **efficient and sustainable** in natural farming.

Best Water Conservation Methods:

✓ **Mulching** – Reduces evaporation by 50%.
✓ **Cover Crops** – Hold moisture and prevent erosion.
✓ **Swales & Trenches** – Capture rainwater and prevent runoff.
✓ **Agroforestry** – Trees improve groundwater levels.

Example: Rajendra Singh, *the Waterman of India*, revived **7 rivers** in Rajasthan through **traditional rainwater harvesting techniques.**

9.5 Economic and Social Benefits of Transitioning

Lower Input Costs – No need for chemical fertilizers or pesticides.
Healthier Soil = Higher Long-Term Yields – Productivity increases over time.
Improved Market Value – Demand for organic and chemical-free food is growing.
Reduced Debt Burden – Farmers avoid expensive loans for synthetic inputs.

Case Study:
Sikkim, India became the **first 100% organic farming state**, increasing farmer incomes and **attracting global buyers** for its chemical-free produce.

9.6 Overcoming Psychological and Social Barriers

"Will this really work?" → Transition **takes time**, but results **improve each season.**
"What will people say?" → Many successful farmers have **proven the benefits** of natural farming.
"What if I lose money?" → **Lower costs + organic premium pricing = long-term profit.**

How to Gain Confidence in Transitioning:

✓ Learn from **successful natural farmers** in your region.

✓ Join **natural farming communities** for support and advice.

✓ Start **small and expand** as you gain experience.

Example: In Maharashtra, India, a community of farmers **collectively shifted to natural farming**, proving that social support accelerates the transition process.

9.7 Conclusion: A Future Rooted in Natural Farming

Transitioning to natural farming is not just about **stopping chemicals**—it's about **rebuilding soil health, protecting biodiversity, and ensuring long-term farm sustainability**.

Key Takeaways:

✓ Transition **gradually** in **three phases**: Soil Restoration → Pest Control → Full Natural Farming.

✓ Use **compost, mulching, and companion planting** to replace synthetic inputs.

✓ **Adopt water conservation techniques** to improve efficiency.

✓ Natural farming is **financially and environmentally sustainable** in the long run.

Final Thought: The shift to natural farming **is a journey, not an overnight change**. With patience, knowledge, and the right techniques, **any farmer can transition successfully and build a thriving, chemical-free farm.**

Chapter 10: Seasonal Planning and Crop Rotation

(Optimizing Farm Productivity Through Smart Planning and Sustainable Practices)

10.1 Introduction: The Importance of Seasonal Planning

Farming is deeply connected to **seasonal cycles**. The success of a farm depends on **planting the right crops at the right time** while ensuring that soil fertility remains intact. Many traditional farmers have long followed **seasonal farming techniques** and **crop rotation methods** to maximize productivity and maintain land health.

However, modern industrial farming has disrupted these natural cycles by **forcing crops to grow out of season**, relying on **synthetic fertilizers and pesticides** instead of working with nature. This results in:

- ✓ **Soil Depletion** – Continuous monocropping depletes soil nutrients.
- ✓ **Increased Pest Problems** – Lack of crop diversity leads to pest infestations.
- ✓ **Water Wastage** – Growing crops outside their natural season requires excessive irrigation.

By adopting **seasonal planning and crop rotation**, farmers can:

- ✓ **Improve soil health** naturally.
- ✓ **Increase yields** by selecting crops suited to each season.
- ✓ **Reduce pests and diseases** without chemical inputs.
- ✓ **Enhance water conservation and farm efficiency**.

This chapter explores **effective seasonal crop planning, crop rotation techniques, and best practices for natural farming.**

10.2 Understanding Seasonal Crop Cycles

Every crop has a **preferred growing season** based on temperature, rainfall, and daylight duration. Seasonal farming means **growing crops when natural conditions are most favourable**, reducing the need for artificial inputs.

10.2.1 Seasonal Crop Categories

Warm-Season Crops*(Spring/Summer)*

- Grow best in **hot temperatures** (above 20°C).
- Require **longer daylight hours**.
- Include: Corn, tomatoes, peppers, cucumbers, okra, and watermelon.

Cool-Season Crops*(Fall/Winter)*

- Grow well in **mild or cold temperatures** (below 20°C).
- Can tolerate **frost and shorter daylight hours**.
- Include: Carrots, cabbage, lettuce, spinach, broccoli, and onions.

Monsoon Crops*(Rainy Season – Tropical Regions)*

- Thrive in **high humidity** and **wet soil conditions**.
- Include: Rice, millet, pigeon peas, green gram, and gourds.

Perennial Crops*(Year-Round Growing)*

- Do not require replanting every year.
- Include: Fruit trees (mango, guava, citrus), moringa, and coffee.

Example: In India, rice and pulses are grown in the monsoon, while wheat and mustard are planted in the winter season.

10.3 The Benefits of Seasonal Crop Planning

10.3.1 Higher Yields with Lower Inputs

- Crops grow **stronger and healthier** when planted in their natural season.
- Less reliance on synthetic fertilizers and pesticides.

10.3.2 Water Conservation

- Seasonal crops **require less irrigation** because they thrive in natural rainfall patterns.

10.3.3 Pest and Disease Reduction

- Out-of-season crops are **weaker and more prone to disease**.
- Proper seasonal planning **interrupts pest life cycles**.

10.3.4 Improved Soil Health

- Rotating crops seasonally **prevents nutrient depletion** and **reduces soil fatigue**.

Example: A farmer growing **lettuce in summer** will struggle with heat stress and pests, whereas **growing lettuce in winter** results in **higher yields with fewer problems**.

10.4 What is Crop Rotation?

Crop rotation is the practice of **growing different types of crops in the same field in successive seasons** to improve soil fertility and prevent pest build-up.

In monoculture farming, the same crop is grown year after year, depleting soil nutrients and attracting pests.

In crop rotation, different crops are grown in a planned sequence, allowing the soil to recover naturally.

10.5 The Benefits of Crop Rotation

- ✓ **Improves Soil Fertility** – Legumes (like beans and peas) **fix nitrogen in the soil**, reducing the need for synthetic fertilizers.
- ✓ **Reduces Pest and Disease Risk** – Changing crops each season **disrupts the life cycle of pests and pathogens.**
- ✓ **Enhances Water Use Efficiency** – Deep-rooted crops **pull nutrients and moisture from deeper soil layers**, improving water retention.
- ✓ **Prevents Weed Growth** – Crop rotation helps **suppress weeds naturally**.

Example: Rotating **corn (a nitrogen-consuming crop) with beans (a nitrogen-fixing crop)** reduces fertilizer requirements and improves yield.

10.6 The Four-Year Crop Rotation Plan

A **simple four-year crop rotation** is an excellent method for maintaining soil health.

Year	Crop Type	Purpose
Year 1	**Legumes (Beans, Peas, Lentils, Clover)**	Fix nitrogen in soil
Year 2	**Leafy Vegetables (Cabbage, Lettuce, Spinach)**	Use nitrogen, improve organic matter
Year 3	**Fruiting Crops (Tomatoes, Peppers, Squash, Cucumbers)**	Use soil nutrients efficiently
Year 4	**Root Crops (Carrots, Onions, Radish, Garlic)**	Aerate soil, prevent compaction

After Year 4, the cycle repeats, ensuring **long-term soil fertility and balanced nutrition**.

Example: In Japan, farmers rotate **rice, soybeans, wheat, and vegetables** to **prevent soil degradation.**

10.7 Best Practices for Seasonal Planning & Crop Rotation

10.7.1 Identify Your Growing Seasons

- Understand the **climatic conditions of your region**.
- Refer to local **agricultural calendars** for the best planting times.

10.7.2 Plan Crop Rotations in Advance

- Choose **legumes before heavy-feeding crops** to naturally enrich the soil.

- Rotate **deep-rooted and shallow-rooted crops** to improve soil structure.

10.7.3 Use Cover Crops in Off-Seasons

- Plant **green manure crops** (clover, alfalfa) to **prevent soil erosion and add organic matter**.

10.7.4 Companion Planting for Extra Benefits

- Plant **marigolds near tomatoes** to **repel pests.**
- Grow **corn with beans** (beans fix nitrogen, corn provides support).

10.7.5 Keep Records of Planting & Harvesting

- Maintain a **farm journal** to track **seasonal crop performance** and **pest/disease patterns.**

10.8 Case Studies: Farmers Using Seasonal Planning and Crop Rotation Successfully

Case Study 1: Organic Wheat Farming in Canada

- Farmers rotate **wheat, clover, and alfalfa**, improving **yields and soil fertility** without synthetic fertilizers.

Case Study 2: Tomato Farmers in Italy

- Seasonal tomato growers follow a **crop rotation system with basil, carrots, and onions**, reducing **soil-borne diseases and increasing profits**.

Case Study 3: Rice-Duck Farming in Japan

- Farmers integrate **ducks in flooded rice fields**, reducing **pest pressure and naturally fertilizing the soil.**

10.9 Conclusion: The Future of Smart Farming

Seasonal crop planning and crop rotation are **simple yet powerful techniques** that every farmer should adopt. By **aligning crop cycles with nature**, farmers can **increase yields, protect soil health, and reduce dependency on external inputs**.

Key Takeaways:

✓**Growing crops in the right season** reduces stress and increases productivity.
✓**Rotating crops** improves soil fertility and controls pests naturally.
✓**Cover crops and companion planting** enhance biodiversity and soil health.
✓**Keeping records and planning ahead** helps optimize farm efficiency.

Final Thought: Smart planning leads to a **healthier farm, better yields, and a more sustainable future.**

Chapter 11: Livestock Integration in Natural Farming

(Creating a Balanced and Self-Sustaining Farm Ecosystem)

11.1 Introduction: The Role of Livestock in Natural Farming

In modern industrial agriculture, livestock and crop farming are often treated as separate entities. However, traditional farming systems **integrated animals with crops**, creating **self-sustaining ecosystems** where both benefited from each other.

Livestock integration in natural farming restores this balance, allowing animals to contribute to **soil fertility, weed control, and pest management**, while benefiting from **natural feed and grazing**. Instead of being seen as a burden, livestock can become an **essential component** of a thriving farm.

Benefits of Livestock Integration

- ✓ **Enriches Soil Fertility** – Animal manure provides organic nutrients, reducing the need for fertilizers.
- ✓ **Reduces Weeds and Pests** – Chickens, ducks, and goats control weeds and insects naturally.
- ✓ **Improves Farm Sustainability** – Reduces external feed and fertilizer costs.
- ✓ **Enhances Biodiversity** – Supports a diverse ecosystem with plants, animals, and microorganisms.

This chapter explores **best practices for integrating livestock into natural farming** while ensuring **ethical and sustainable animal management**.

11.2 Choosing the Right Livestock for Your Farm

Not all livestock are suitable for every farm. The right choice depends on **farm size, climate, available resources, and crop type**.

Livestock Type	Benefits in Natural Farming	Best Suited For
Cows & Buffaloes	Provide dung and urine for compost and biofertilizers like Jeevamrit	Dairy farms, large-scale farms
Goats & Sheep	Natural weed controllers, produce manure, adapt to dry conditions	Agroforestry, dryland farming
Chickens & Ducks	Eat pests, aerate soil, fertilize fields	Vegetable farms, rice paddies
Pigs	Convert farm waste into manure, help in composting	Small-scale mixed farms
Bees	Pollinate crops, produce honey	Fruit orchards, vegetable farms
Fish (Aquaponics)	Provide nutrient-rich water for plants	Integrated rice or vegetable farming

Example: Farmers in Japan integrate **ducks in rice fields**, where ducks **eat insects and weeds while fertilizing the water**, reducing chemical input costs.

11.3 Natural Livestock Management: Ethical and Sustainable Practices

Animals in natural farming are **treated with care and respect**, ensuring their well-being while maximizing their benefits to the farm.

11.3.1 Free-Range & Rotational Grazing

Instead of keeping animals in confined spaces, **rotational grazing** allows them to roam freely while fertilizing the land.

How It Works:

- Divide grazing land into sections (**paddocks**).
- Rotate livestock across these sections to allow **soil recovery and pasture regrowth**.
- Prevents **overgrazing**, maintains **soil fertility**, and improves **grass regeneration**.

Benefits:

✓ Reduces soil erosion by preventing overgrazing.

✓ Improves carbon sequestration in soil.
✓ Enhances the nutritional quality of pasture for animals.

Example: In Africa, rotational grazing has **restored degraded land**, turning dry pastures into **lush grazing fields**.

11.3.2 Manure Management: Turning Waste into Fertilizer

Animal manure is **a natural, nutrient-rich fertilizer** that enhances soil health. Instead of allowing manure to pollute water sources, it is **composted and used to enrich crops**.

Best Practices for Manure Use in Natural Farming:

- **Jeevamrit (Microbial Soil Booster):** Fermented cow dung and urine solution improves soil microbial activity.
- **Vermicomposting with Manure:** Earthworms break down manure into **nutrient-rich humus**.
- **Biochar with Manure:** Mixing manure with **biochar** reduces methane emissions and improves **nutrient retention**.

Example: Farmers in India use cow dung to make **Jeevamrit**, eliminating the need for synthetic fertilizers.

11.3.3 Livestock for Weed and Pest Control

Goats: Naturally clear weeds and overgrown areas, reducing the need for herbicides.
Ducks: Eat insects in rice paddies, eliminating pests **without pesticides**.
Chickens: Scratch and aerate soil while eating insects and larvae.

Example: In vineyards, **sheep graze between grapevines, controlling weeds and fertilizing the soil simultaneously**.

11.4 Integrating Livestock with Crop Systems

11.4.1 Cows & Buffaloes: The Backbone of Regenerative Farms

- Provide **high-quality manure** for soil enrichment.
- Urine is used in **organic fertilizers like Jeevamrit and Beejamrit**.
- Used for **draught power**, reducing dependence on fuel-driven machinery.

Example: In Brazil, **integrating cattle with crops** has increased soil fertility, leading to **higher yields without synthetic fertilizers**.

11.4.2 Poultry: The Natural Pest Controllers

- Chickens and ducks **eat insects, weeds, and leftover grains.**
- Chicken droppings **enhance compost piles**, making them **nutrient-rich**.
- Moving chicken coops across fields **evenly distributes manure**.

Example: Farmers in the Philippines integrate **ducks in vegetable fields**, reducing pests by **60% without pesticides.**

11.4.3 Beekeeping: Pollination & Honey Production

Bees are **critical for crop pollination**, increasing fruit and vegetable yields.

How to Integrate Bees into a Farm:

- Plant **flowering crops** like sunflowers, mustard, and herbs to attract bees.
- Maintain **natural hedgerows** as bee habitats.
- Avoid chemical pesticides that harm bee colonies.

Example: Apple farmers in Himachal Pradesh, India, **increased fruit set by 40%** after introducing honeybee colonies to their farms.

11.4.4 Aquaponics: Fish & Plant Co-Growth

Aquaponics combines **fish farming with vegetable production**.

How It Works:

- Fish waste **fertilizes plants** with nitrogen and phosphorus.
- Plants **clean the water**, which is cycled back to the fish tank.
- Works best for **leafy greens, tomatoes, and herbs**.

Example: In Thailand, farmers integrate **catfish ponds with vegetable farms**, creating a **self-sufficient food system**.

11.5 Economic and Environmental Benefits of Livestock Integration

Environmental Benefits:

✓ Reduces **synthetic fertilizer use**, preventing soil degradation.
✓ Increases **biodiversity**, balancing farm ecosystems.
✓ Prevents **land degradation** through rotational grazing.

Economic Benefits:

✓ Generates **multiple income streams** (milk, eggs, honey, manure sales).

✓ Reduces **feed costs** through natural grazing.
✓ Increases **crop yields** through natural fertilization.

Example: In Europe, **silvopasture systems (combining trees with livestock grazing)** increased **farmer incomes by 30%** while improving **soil carbon storage**.

11.6 Conclusion: A Holistic Approach to Farming

Integrating livestock into natural farming **creates a balanced, sustainable, and productive ecosystem**. By **using animals for soil enrichment, weed control, and pest management**, farmers can reduce costs while improving farm resilience.

Key Takeaways:

✓**Cows, goats, chickens, and ducks** enhance farm sustainability.
✓**Manure is a natural fertilizer** that improves soil fertility.
✓**Rotational grazing protects land** and **reduces soil erosion**.
✓**Bees, fish, and poultry offer additional income streams.**

Final Thought: A farm without livestock is **missing a key component of natural farming**. By integrating animals, farmers can **build a self-sustaining system that benefits both the land and the people**.

Chapter 12: Urban and Small-Scale Natural Farming

(Bringing Sustainable Agriculture to Cities and Small Spaces)

12.1 Introduction: The Growing Need for Urban and Small-Scale Farming

As cities expand and farmland shrinks, the need for **urban and small-scale farming** has never been greater. With rising food prices, concerns over **chemical-laden produce**, and a growing interest in **self-sufficiency**, more people are turning to **natural farming methods in small spaces.**

Why Urban and Small-Scale Farming Matters:

- **Reduces dependency** on industrial food systems.
- **Utilizes available space** in backyards, rooftops, and balconies.
- **Produces fresh, chemical-free food** at home.
- **Builds resilient communities** with local food networks.

Even in **small backyards, rooftops, or apartment balconies**, people can practice **natural farming principles**—creating **self-sustaining ecosystems** that mimic traditional farms on a **miniature scale**.

Example: In Havana, Cuba, urban farmers use **rooftops and vacant lots** to grow organic vegetables, providing **70% of the city's fresh food**.

12.2 Principles of Urban and Small-Scale Natural Farming

Just like in large farms, **urban and small-scale natural farming** follows these core principles:

✓ **Minimal Soil Disturbance** – No tilling; use compost and mulching instead.
✓ **Chemical-Free Inputs** – No synthetic fertilizers or pesticides.
✓ **Diverse Planting (Polyculture)** – Grow multiple crops together for balance.
✓ **Encouraging Pollinators** – Bees, butterflies, and birds help in crop productivity.
✓ **Water Conservation** – Use rainwater harvesting and drip irrigation.

Even in **limited spaces**, farmers can apply **organic, regenerative farming techniques** to grow **healthy food naturally**.

12.3 Types of Urban and Small-Scale Natural Farming

12.3.1 Backyard and Home Gardening

Small plots of land **can be transformed** into thriving **organic gardens** with **compost, mulching, and natural fertilizers**.

Best Practices:

- **Use raised beds** to maximize space.
- **Practice companion planting** to improve soil fertility.
- **Apply mulching** to retain moisture and reduce weeds.

Example: In India, thousands of families are growing **organic vegetables** in their backyards using **vermicompost and natural sprays** instead of chemicals.

12.3.2 Rooftop Farming

In cities where **land is scarce**, rooftops **offer the perfect space** for growing food naturally.

Best Crops for Rooftop Farming:
Tomatoes, Lettuce, Peppers, Eggplants, Cucumbers, Herbs (Basil, Mint, Coriander)

Techniques Used in Rooftop Farming:

- **Container Gardening** – Grow crops in pots, grow bags, and wooden crates.
- **Vertical Gardening** – Use wall-mounted planters to **maximize space**.
- **Drip Irrigation** – Efficient water use with minimal waste.

Example: In New York City, **Brooklyn Grange** operates the world's **largest rooftop farm**, producing **50,000 pounds of organic produce annually**.

12.3.3 Balcony and Terrace Gardening

Even **small balconies** can become **mini natural farms** with proper planning.

Essential Elements for Balcony Farming:

✓ **Containers** – Use pots, wooden crates, or recycled materials.
✓ **Soil & Compost** – Maintain rich organic soil with kitchen waste composting.
✓ **Sunlight & Water** – Ensure **4–6 hours of sunlight** and use **self-watering containers**.

Example: Many urban residents in Japan **grow organic vegetables on balconies** using compost bins, **turning food scraps into rich fertilizer**.

12.3.4 Vertical Farming (Space-Saving Agriculture)

Vertical farming **maximizes productivity in small spaces** by growing crops **upwards** instead of spreading them out.

Techniques Used in Vertical Farming:

- **Hanging Gardens** – Use suspended planters for herbs and strawberries.
- **Green Walls** – Vertical panels filled with soil for dense vegetable planting.
- **Hydroponics & Aquaponics** – Soil-less growing techniques for **small urban spaces**.

Example: In Singapore, **vertical farms grow 10 times more food per square foot** than traditional farming, supplying **fresh greens to local markets**.

12.3.5 Community and Guerrilla Gardening

Urban residents often **transform vacant lots, sidewalks, and public spaces** into **community gardens**, producing **local, chemical-free food**.

Benefits of Community Gardens:

✓ **Strengthens food security** in urban areas.
✓ **Encourages people to grow their own food** naturally.

✓ **Builds green spaces** that improve city air quality.

Example: The "Dig In" project in the UK **turned abandoned land into thriving organic farms**, feeding local neighbourhoods.

12.4 Natural Soil Enrichment in Small-Scale Farming

Since urban soil is often **degraded or polluted**, it is essential to **improve soil health** naturally.

Best Practices for Healthy Soil:

✓ **Vermicomposting:** Convert kitchen scraps into **nutrient-rich compost.**
✓ **Mulching:** Cover soil with **dry leaves or straw** to retain moisture.
✓ **Natural Fertilizers:** Use **cow dung, compost tea, and biochar** to enrich soil.

Example: Cuban urban farmers restored **barren city soil using compost and natural amendments**, turning **urban wastelands into fertile gardens.**

12.5 Water Conservation for Small-Scale Farmers

Since **water is limited in cities**, urban farmers must use **efficient irrigation techniques**.

Best Water Conservation Methods:

- **Rainwater Harvesting** – Collect and store rainwater for irrigation.
- **Drip Irrigation** – Slow water release **directly at plant roots**.
- **Self-Watering Containers** – Reduce water waste using built-in reservoirs.

Example: Rooftop farmers in Mumbai use **rainwater harvesting** to grow vegetables, **reducing water costs by 40%.**

12.6 Pest and Disease Control Without Chemicals

Urban farmers can **avoid pesticides** by using **natural pest control methods**.

Best Natural Pest Control Strategies:

✓ **Companion Planting:** Grow basil with tomatoes to **repel whiteflies**.
✓ **Natural Predators:** Encourage ladybugs to eat aphids.

- ✓ **Homemade Sprays:** Use **neem oil, garlic-chili spray, or cow urine tonic.**

Example: Urban gardeners in Toronto use **marigolds and companion plants** to **keep pests away naturally**.

12.7 Economic and Social Benefits of Urban Natural Farming

- ✓ **Saves Money:** Reduces grocery costs by **growing organic food at home.**
- ✓ **Promotes Self-Sufficiency:** Encourages people to **grow food instead of buying it**.
- ✓ **Improves Sustainability:** Reduces **food transportation emissions.**
- ✓ **Creates Community Bonds:** Brings neighborhoods together through **shared farming spaces.**

Case Study: In Detroit, USA, urban farming transformed **vacant lots into organic vegetable gardens**, helping residents access **fresh, affordable food.**

12.8 Conclusion: The Future of Small-Scale and Urban Farming

As cities grow, **small-scale natural farming will play a key role** in feeding communities **without relying on chemical-heavy agriculture.**

Key Takeaways:

✓**Rooftop, backyard, and balcony farms** make organic food accessible.

✓**Vertical farming and hydroponics** maximize small spaces.

✓**Rainwater harvesting and drip irrigation** improve water efficiency.

✓**Compost and organic mulching** create healthy soil.

✓**Urban farming builds food security and self-sufficiency.**

Final Thought:Anyone, anywhere, can grow food naturally—whether in a backyard, rooftop, or even an apartment window.

Chapter 13: Natural Farming and Climate Resilience

(Building Sustainable Agriculture to Withstand Climate Change)

13.1 Introduction: The Need for Climate-Resilient Farming

Climate change is one of the **biggest threats to global food security**. Rising temperatures, erratic rainfall, prolonged droughts, and extreme weather events are making traditional farming **increasingly difficult**.

How Climate Change Affects Agriculture:

✓ **Heat Stress** – Higher temperatures reduce crop yields and livestock productivity.
✓ **Water Scarcity** – Drought limit irrigation and decrease soil moisture.
✓ **Extreme Weather** – Floods, storms, and frost damage crops.
✓ **Pest & Disease Surges** – Warmer conditions lead to increased pest outbreaks.

To combat these challenges, farmers must **adapt and build resilience.** Natural farming offers a **sustainable solution**, helping farmers grow food while **protecting soil, conserving water, and restoring ecosystems.**

Why Natural Farming is Climate-Resilient:

- **Improves soil structure** to withstand droughts and floods.
- **Enhances biodiversity** to prevent pest outbreaks.
- **Reduces dependency** on synthetic inputs that degrade land.
- **Sequesters carbon** in soil, mitigating climate change.

Example: In Andhra Pradesh, India, farmers practicing **Zero Budget Natural Farming (ZBNF)** saw **higher yields and better drought resistance** than chemical-based farms.

13.2 How Natural Farming Improves Climate Resilience

Natural farming strengthens the **three pillars of climate-resilient agriculture**:

13.2.1 Soil Health and Carbon Sequestration

Healthy soil **absorbs and retains moisture**, reducing the impact of droughts and floods. Natural farming enhances soil health by:

✓ **No-Till Farming** – Prevents soil erosion and increases organic matter.
✓ **Mulching** – Reduces water evaporation and suppresses weeds.
✓ **Composting & Manure Use** – Feeds soil microbes, improving structure and fertility.
✓ **Carbon Sequestration:** Natural farming **captures carbon from the air** and stores it in soil, reducing CO_2 levels.

Example: Studies show that **agroforestry and organic farming** can **sequester up to 3 tons of CO_2 per hectare annually**.

13.2.2 Water Conservation and Drought Resilience

Water shortages are a major challenge for farmers worldwide. Natural farming improves **water retention** and reduces dependency on irrigation.

Key Water Conservation Methods:

- **Rainwater Harvesting** – Captures and stores water for dry seasons.
- **Whapasa (Moisture Balance Concept)** – Maintains soil moisture **without over-irrigation**.
- **Cover Crops & Agroforestry** – Trees and deep-rooted plants **hold groundwater** and prevent evaporation.

Example: In Rajasthan, India, farmers restored dried-up lands using **traditional rainwater harvesting systems**, making their farms productive again.

13.2.3 Biodiversity for Pest and Disease Resistance

Monoculture farming is highly **vulnerable to climate-related pest and disease outbreaks**. Natural farming encourages **biodiversity**, creating **self-sustaining ecosystems** that regulate pests naturally.

Techniques for Pest & Disease Resistance:

✓ **Companion Planting** – Certain plants repel pests (e.g., marigolds deter nematodes).
✓ **Livestock Integration** – Ducks in rice fields eat insects and fertilize soil.
✓ **Encouraging Natural Predators** – Birds, ladybugs, and frogs keep pest populations low.

Example: In Kenya, farmers using **push-pull technology** (desmodium repelling pests, napier grass attracting them) saw **80% fewer pest outbreaks** compared to monoculture farms.

13.3 The Role of Agroforestry in Climate Resilience

Agroforestry—the integration of **trees, crops, and livestock**—is one of the most **climate-resilient farming methods**.

Benefits of Agroforestry:

✓**Prevents Soil Erosion** – Tree roots bind soil and prevent degradation.
✓**Shades Crops from Extreme Heat** – Reduces heat stress and evaporation.
✓**Improves Water Retention** – Deep-rooted trees bring up groundwater.
✓**Provides Additional Income** – Fruits, nuts, timber, and medicinal plants.

Example: In Africa's Sahel region, farmers use **agroforestry to restore degraded land**, bringing **once-barren fields back to life**.

13.4 Reducing Chemical Dependence for a Sustainable Future

Industrial agriculture relies on:

- ✓ **Synthetic Fertilizers** – Release greenhouse gases like nitrous oxide.
- ✓ **Pesticides & Herbicides** – Kill beneficial microbes and pollinators.
- ✓ **Heavy Machinery** – Causes **soil compaction and CO_2 emissions.**

Natural Farming Eliminates These Problems:

- **Organic compost & biofertilizers** replace synthetic fertilizers.
- **Neem oil, cow urine sprays, and companion planting** replace pesticides.
- **Livestock integration** eliminates the need for synthetic manure.

Example: Sikkim, India, became the **first 100% organic farming state**, reducing **chemical dependency while increasing soil fertility**.

13.5 Economic and Social Benefits of Climate-Resilient Farming

Economic Benefits:

✓**Lower Input Costs** – No need for chemical fertilizers, pesticides, or expensive machinery.
✓**Higher Long-Term Yields** – Healthy soil leads to **stable and sustainable production**.
✓**Diverse Income Sources** – Trees, livestock, and medicinal plants **provide multiple revenue streams**.

Social Benefits:

✓**Improved Farmer Livelihoods** – Reduces debt and financial risks.
✓**Community Resilience** – Encourages local food systems and self-sufficiency.
✓**Better Nutrition & Health** – Reduces chemical residues in food.

Example: Farmers in Nepal using **organic farming methods** reported **higher incomes and better food security** than those relying on chemical-based farming.

13.6 Case Studies: Farmers Adapting to Climate Change with Natural Farming

Case Study 1: Regenerative Agriculture in Australia

- Farmers suffering from **severe droughts** switched to **holistic grazing and cover cropping, restoring soil moisture and doubling productivity**.

Case Study 2: Traditional Rice Farming in Japan

- Japanese farmers **integrated ducks into rice fields**, reducing pest outbreaks and eliminating pesticides **while increasing rice yields by 20%**.

Case Study 3: Agroforestry in Brazil

- Small farmers in Brazil planted **fruit and nut trees alongside crops**, improving **drought resistance and generating additional income**.

13.7 The Future of Climate-Resilient Natural Farming

With climate change intensifying, **natural farming is no longer an option—it is a necessity**. By **restoring ecosystems, conserving water, and reducing emissions**, natural farming **not only adapts to climate change but actively fights it**.

Key Takeaways:

✓**Healthy soil stores carbon**, reducing climate impact.
✓**Water conservation techniques** make farms more resilient to droughts.
✓**Biodiversity controls pests naturally**, reducing chemical dependence.
✓**Agroforestry prevents erosion and improves water retention.**
✓**Sustainable practices ensure long-term farm productivity and food security.**

Final Thought: The future of farming must be **climate-smart and nature-driven**—and natural farming provides the roadmap to that future.

Chapter 14: Economic and Social Impact of Natural Farming

(How Sustainable Agriculture Transforms Communities and Economies)

14.1 Introduction: The Far-Reaching Benefits of Natural Farming

Natural farming is more than just an agricultural practice—it is a **powerful economic and social movement** that improves the well-being of farmers, consumers, and entire communities. By eliminating chemical inputs, reducing costs, and improving soil health, natural farming provides **financial stability** for farmers while producing **healthier food** for society.

In this chapter, we explore the **economic and social benefits** of natural farming, focusing on how it:

- ✓ **Reduces farming costs and debt cycles.**
- ✓ **Boosts farmer incomes through organic and local markets.**
- ✓ **Improves food security and community resilience.**
- ✓ **Creates employment opportunities and strengthens rural economies.**

Example: In Andhra Pradesh, India, farmers who switched to **Zero Budget Natural Farming (ZBNF)doubled their profits** while eliminating input costs.

14.2 The Economic Advantages of Natural Farming

14.2.1 Lower Farming Costs and Financial Independence

Conventional farming requires expensive inputs:

- ✓ Chemical fertilizers
- ✓ Pesticides and herbicides
- ✓ Hybrid or GMO seeds
- ✓ High irrigation costs

Natural farming eliminates these costs by using:

- ✓ **Compost and manure** instead of synthetic fertilizers.
- ✓ **Neem, cow urine, and bio-pesticides** instead of chemicals.
- ✓ **Indigenous seeds**, reducing dependency on corporations.
- ✓ **Rainwater harvesting and moisture retention techniques** to cut irrigation costs.

Example: A farmer in Maharashtra saved **50,000 rupees ($600) per year** by switching from chemical fertilizers to farm-made Jeevamrit.

14.2.2 Higher Profit Margins Through Organic Markets

Consumers are **increasingly willing to pay more** for chemical-free food.

Why Organic and Natural Produce Earns More:

- People prefer **healthier, pesticide-free food.**
- Organic products **sell at a premium price** in urban markets.
- Direct-to-consumer sales (farmer's markets, community-supported agriculture) **eliminate middlemen.**

Example: In Sikkim, India's first **100% organic state**, farmers' incomes **increased by 20-30%** due to high demand for chemical-free food.

14.2.3 Reduced Farmer Debt and Financial Risk

Many farmers are trapped in a **cycle of debt** due to high input costs.

Natural farming provides financial stability by:
✓**Eliminating costly inputs**, reducing reliance on loans.
✓**Ensuring consistent soil fertility**, leading to stable yields.
✓**Reducing crop failure risks** through diversified farming.

Example: In Punjab, India, farmers who transitioned to **natural farming avoided debt cycles**, while those dependent on chemicals **faced financial distress due to increasing costs.**

14.2.4 Job Creation and Rural Employment

Natural farming **creates more jobs** compared to industrialized, mechanized farming.

How Natural Farming Generates Employment:

- ✓ **Encourages labor-intensive practices** like composting and agroforestry.
- ✓ **Creates small-scale organic processing businesses** (e.g., handmade organic fertilizers, honey production).
- ✓ **Promotes eco-tourism and farm-based businesses** (farm-to-table restaurants, educational farms).

Example: In Indonesia, agroforestry projects employing natural farming techniques **created thousands of jobs** in rural areas while restoring degraded land.

14.3 Social Impact: How Natural Farming Strengthens Communities

14.3.1 Improved Food Security and Nutrition

Conventional farming focuses on high-yield crops like wheat, corn, and rice—often lacking diversity and nutrition.

Natural farming promotes food diversity, ensuring:

✓**Chemical-free, nutrient-rich food** for families and communities.

✓**More variety** through intercropping and polyculture.

✓**Resilient local food systems** that reduce dependence on imported food.

Example: In Kenya, small-scale farmers practicing permaculture **produced diverse foods year-round**, improving local nutrition.

14.3.2 Health Benefits for Farmers and Consumers

The dangers of conventional farming:

- ✓ Pesticide exposure leads to **cancer, respiratory diseases, and neurological disorders.**
- ✓ Synthetic fertilizers degrade soil, making food **less nutritious.**
- ✓ Farmers using chemicals **suffer from high medical costs** due to long-term health issues.

How Natural Farming Improves Health:

- ✓ Reduces pesticide-related diseases.
- ✓ Produces **nutrient-dense food** free of toxins.
- ✓ Lowers healthcare costs for farmers and consumers.

Example: Studies in Sri Lanka showed that **pesticide-free farming reduced cases of kidney disease** among rural farmers.

14.3.3 Strengthening Rural Communities

Natural farming encourages **community collaboration and shared knowledge**, making farming more **socially sustainable.**

How Natural Farming Unites Communities:

✓ Farmers **share indigenous knowledge and traditional techniques**.

✓**Community seed banks** preserve native crop varieties.

✓**Women's cooperatives** benefit from small-scale organic farming projects.

Example: In Tamil Nadu, India, women-led farmer groups practice **collective natural farming**, reducing costs and increasing incomes for entire villages.

14.3.4 Women Empowerment in Farming

Women play a **vital role in natural farming**, managing home gardens, composting, and seed preservation.

Natural Farming Creates Opportunities for Women:

- ✓ **Lower input costs** enable women farmers to start small businesses.

- ✓ **Organic food production** creates home-based income sources (e.g., selling homemade pickles, organic vegetables).
- ✓ **Women's cooperatives** enable better land ownership and decision-making power.

Example: In Nepal, women's farming groups using natural methods increased household incomes by **35%** while improving food security.

14.4 Natural Farming and Sustainable Development Goals (SDGs)

Natural farming contributes to multiple **United Nations Sustainable Development Goals (SDGs)**:

Sustainable Development Goal	How Natural Farming Helps
Zero Hunger (SDG 2)	Increases food production sustainably.
Clean Water (SDG 6)	Prevents pesticide and fertilizer contamination.
Good Health (SDG 3)	Provides chemical-free, nutrient-rich food.
Climate Action (SDG 13)	Sequesters carbon and improves soil health.
Decent Work & Economic Growth (SDG 8)	Creates jobs in sustainable agriculture.

Example: The FAO (Food and Agriculture Organization) promotes **agroecology and natural farming** as solutions to meet global food and environmental challenges.

14.5 Challenges and the Way Forward

While natural farming has **proven economic and social benefits**, challenges remain:

Barriers to Widespread Adoption:

- ✓ **Government policies often favor industrial farming.**
- ✓ **Limited access to organic markets and fair pricing.**
- ✓ **Lack of education on natural farming techniques.**

Solutions for a Sustainable Future:

- ✓ **Stronger farmer networks** to promote knowledge-sharing.
- ✓ **Government support for organic and regenerative farming.**
- ✓ **Increased consumer awareness** to support chemical-free food.

Example: Countries like Bhutan aim to become **100% organic**, proving that government policies can support **sustainable farming at a national level**.

14.6 Conclusion: A Prosperous and Sustainable Future with Natural Farming

Natural farming is **not just about agriculture—it's about building a better world**. It empowers farmers financially, strengthens communities, improves human health, and supports environmental sustainability.

Key Takeaways:

✓**Reduces farming costs and debt cycles.**
✓**Increases profitability through organic markets.**
✓**Improves food security and community resilience.**
✓**Creates jobs and empowers women in farming.**
✓**Supports global sustainability goals (SDGs).**

Final Thought: The shift to natural farming is **not just a return to traditional wisdom—it is the future of sustainable agriculture and a better society.**

Chapter 15: The Future of Natural Farming

(Innovations, Challenges, and the Path Forward for Sustainable Agriculture)

15.1 Introduction: The Evolution of Natural Farming

Natural farming has been practiced for centuries, long before industrial agriculture introduced synthetic fertilizers, pesticides, and mechanization. However, with increasing concerns about **climate change, soil degradation, and food security**, the world is now **returning to nature-based solutions** for sustainable agriculture.

Why the Future of Farming is Natural Farming:

- ✓ **Soil health is declining** due to excessive chemical use—natural farming restores it.
- ✓ **Water scarcity is increasing**—natural methods improve moisture retention.
- ✓ **Pesticide resistance and biodiversity loss** are worsening—natural farming encourages ecological balance.
- ✓ **Farmers are trapped in debt cycles**—natural farming reduces costs and increases self-sufficiency.

Example: The FAO (Food and Agriculture Organization) now promotes **agroecology and regenerative farming** as solutions for global food production.

This chapter explores the **future of natural farming**, including **emerging trends, challenges, technological advancements, and the role of policies and global movements**.

15.2 Emerging Trends in Natural Farming

15.2.1 Agroecology and Regenerative Agriculture

The future of farming is **regenerative**—restoring ecosystems while producing food.

Key Elements of Regenerative Agriculture:

- **Building soil organic matter** through composting and cover cropping.
- **Enhancing biodiversity** by integrating trees, livestock, and crops.
- **Reducing carbon footprint** by minimizing tilling and synthetic inputs.

Example: In the USA, regenerative farming is now supported by **large food companies** like General Mills, which plan to transition millions of acres to sustainable practices.

15.2.2 Permaculture and Sustainable Urban Farming

Urban populations are growing, and **small-scale farming innovations** will be crucial in the future.

Future Urban Farming Trends:

- **Rooftop farms and vertical gardens** to grow food in cities.
- **Community-supported agriculture (CSA)**, where people buy directly from farmers.
- **Permaculture food forests**, where multiple plant species grow together in harmony.

Example: Singapore has developed **vertical farms** to grow food in limited space, ensuring **fresh local produce without harming the environment**.

15.2.3 Climate-Smart Farming

With unpredictable weather patterns, farmers must **adapt to climate change** using **resilient techniques**.

Climate-Resilient Natural Farming Practices:

- ✓ **Drought-resistant crops** (millets, sorghum, moringa)
- ✓ **Agroforestry for cooling effects**
- ✓ **Rainwater harvesting and moisture-retention farming**

Example: In Rajasthan, India, farmers are **reviving traditional rainwater storage techniques** to make farming drought-resistant.

15.3 The Role of Technology in Natural Farming

While natural farming is based on **traditional knowledge**, modern technology can **enhance and scale it globally**.

15.3.1 AI and Data-Driven Natural Farming

How AI and Data Can Improve Natural Farming:

- **Precision agriculture**—using drones and sensors to track soil moisture.
- **AI-powered pest detection**—monitoring crops to predict outbreaks before they happen.
- **Blockchain for farm-to-table tracking**—ensuring transparency in organic food production.

Example: In Brazil, AI tools analyze**soil health** and suggest **composting and crop rotation strategies**, reducing **chemical dependency**.

15.3.2 Biofertilizers and Microbial Technology

Advancements in **soil microbiology** are helping farmers move away from synthetic fertilizers.

Future Innovations in Biofertilizers:

- **Indigenous microbes (IMO)** to enhance soil fertility.
- **Mycorrhizal fungi** to improve nutrient uptake in plants.
- **Liquid compost teas** replacing chemical fertilizers.

Example: Scientists in Japan are developing **biofertilizers from beneficial bacteria**, reducing chemical fertilizer use by 50%.

15.3.3 Renewable Energy in Farming

As energy prices rise, natural farms are shifting to **renewable power sources.**

Sustainable Energy for Natural Farms:

- **Solar-powered irrigation systems**
- **Biogas digesters for farm waste management**
- **Wind-powered grain mills and cold storage**

Example: African farmers are adopting **solar-powered irrigation systems**, reducing reliance on fossil fuels.

15.4 Policy and Government Support for Natural Farming

For natural farming to become mainstream, **governments must create policies that support it**.

15.4.1 Subsidies for Natural Farming

Many governments **subsidize chemical fertilizers and pesticides**, making it harder for farmers to transition. Future policies must:

✓ **Shift subsidies towards organic inputs** (compost, biofertilizers).
✓ **Support farmers during transition periods** to offset yield fluctuations.
✓ **Promote local seed banks** to preserve indigenous crop varieties.

Example: India's Andhra Pradesh state aims to transition **6 million farmers** to **Zero Budget Natural Farming (ZBNF)** by 2030.

15.4.2 Organic Certification and Market Expansion

Many farmers struggle to **sell natural produce** due to **expensive certification processes**. Future solutions include:

✓ **Decentralized certification programs** for small farmers.
✓ **Digital platforms to connect natural farmers with buyers**.

✓ **Incentives for large companies to source from natural farms.**

Example: The European Union now **subsidizes organic farmers** to help them compete with industrial agriculture.

15.4.3 Integrating Natural Farming into Education

To ensure the **future of natural farming**, education systems must include:

✓ **Agroecology and permaculture courses** in schools and universities.
✓ **Farmer-to-farmer training programs.**
✓ **Research on indigenous knowledge and farming techniques.**

Example: In Cuba, universities **teach agroecology as part of the national curriculum**, training thousands of students in sustainable farming.

15.5 Challenges and Solutions for the Future of Natural Farming

Challenges Facing Natural Farming:

✓ **Transition Period Risks** – Farmers may experience **lower yields initially.**
✓ **Lack of Market Access** – Many farmers **struggle to sell their organic produce.**
✓ **Knowledge Gaps** – Younger generations **lack exposure to traditional farming methods.**

Solutions for a Sustainable Future:

✓ **Financial support for farmers** transitioning to natural methods.
✓ **Stronger farmer cooperatives** to share knowledge and resources.
✓ **More research in agroecology** to improve yield stability.

Example: Bhutan's government supports **100% organic farming**, proving that **strong policies can drive sustainable agriculture forward.**

15.6 Conclusion: The Road Ahead for Natural Farming

The **future of agriculture is natural**—but transitioning from **chemical-based industrial farming** to **sustainable, regenerative farming** requires:

✓ **Government policies that prioritize agroecology.**
✓ **Public awareness about the benefits of organic and natural food.**
✓ **Scientific advancements that enhance natural farming techniques.**
✓ **Farmer-led movements to share knowledge and practices.**

Key Takeaways:

✓**Natural farming is the most sustainable way to feed future generations.**

✓**Technology and traditional knowledge must work together** for better farming solutions.

✓**Policy changes, market access, and education** are crucial for growth.

✓**The world is shifting towards agroecology, organic farming, and regenerative agriculture.**

Final Thought: The future of farming must be built on **healthy soil, strong communities, and sustainable practices**—because when we take care of nature, nature takes care of us.

References

1. Altieri, M. A. (1995). *Agroecology: The science of sustainable agriculture.* CRC Press.
2. Anderson, M. D. (2007). The case for organic agriculture. *Food and Agriculture Organization.*
3. Behera, U. K., & France, J. (2007). Integrated farming systems for sustainable agriculture. *Indian Journal of Agronomy, 52*(2), 73–84.
4. Bhattacharyya, R., Kundu, S., Pandey, S. C., Singh, K. P., Gupta, H. S. (2018). Conservation agriculture and soil carbon sequestration. *Soil and Tillage Research, 192*, 10–20. https://doi.org/10.1016/j.still.2018.04.012
5. Bharucha, Z. P., Pretty, J., & Smith, P. (2013). Sustainable intensification and agroecological farming. *Science, 341*(6141), 33–34.
6. Birkhofer, K., Bezemer, T. M., Bloem, J., Bonkowski, M., Christensen, S., Dubois, D., ... & Hedlund, K. (2008). Organic farming and soil biodiversity. *Biological Conservation, 141*(10), 2482–2491.
7. Chand, R. (2017). Doubling farmers' income: Rationale, strategy and action plan. *NITI Aayog, Government of India.*
8. Choudhary, M. L., & Dixit, S. K. (2011). *Organic farming for sustainable horticulture.* Daya Publishing House.
9. Clements, D. R., & Shrestha, A. (2004). *New dimensions in agroecology.* Food Products Press.
10. Das, A., Ghosh, P. K., & Choudhury, B. U. (2013). Organic and conservation agriculture. *Current Science, 104*(10), 1323–1325.
11. Debnath, S., & Ghosh, M. (2022). Farmer-centric innovation in natural farming. *Journal of Eco-Friendly Agriculture, 17*(4), 39–44.
12. Food and Agriculture Organization (FAO). (2018). *The 10 elements of agroecology.* FAO.
13. Food and Agriculture Organization (FAO). (2019). *Scaling up agroecology to achieve the SDGs.* FAO.
14. Fukuoka, M. (1978). *The one-straw revolution: An introduction to natural farming.* Rodale Press.
15. Ghosh, P. K., Ramesh, P., Bandyopadhyay, K. K., Tripathi, A. K., Hati, K. M., & Misra, A. K. (2007). Integrated nutrient management. *Indian Journal of Agronomy, 52*(3), 186–191.
16. Gliessman, S. R. (2007). *Agroecology: The ecology of sustainable food systems* (2nd ed.). CRC Press.
17. Government of India. (2020). *Operational guidelines for Bhartiya Prakritik Krishi Paddhati (BPKP).* Ministry of Agriculture & Farmers Welfare.
18. Indian Council of Agricultural Research (ICAR). (2021). *Natural farming research initiatives.* ICAR.
19. Jackson, L. E., Pascual, U., & Hodgkin, T. (2010). Ecological agriculture and climate change. *Ecological Applications, 20*(1), 18–24.
20. Lal, R. (2004). Soil carbon sequestration impacts on global climate change and food security. *Science, 304*(5677), 1623–1627. https://doi.org/10.1126/science.1097396
21. Lin, B. B. (2011). Resilience in agriculture through crop diversification: Adaptive management for environmental change. *Bioscience, 61*(3), 183–193. https://doi.org/10.1525/bio.2011.61.3.4

22. Mahapatra, I. C. (1994). Farming system research: Challenges and opportunities. *Indian Journal of Agronomy, 39*(1), 1–12.
23. Mishra, S., & Singh, R. (2021). Natural farming: Evidence from Andhra Pradesh. *Azim Premji University Working Paper Series*.
24. Ministry of Agriculture and Farmers Welfare. (2017). *Paramparagat Krishi Vikas Yojana (PKVY) guidelines*. Government of India.
25. Nair, K. P. P. (2010). *The agronomy and economy of important tree crops of the developing world*. Elsevier.
26. National Institute of Agricultural Extension Management (MANAGE). (2022). *DAESI programme guidelines*. MANAGE.
27. Pandey, S., & Singh, R. K. (2019). Economics of natural farming in India. *Economic & Political Weekly, 54*(16), 43–49.
28. Paroda, R. (2020). Transforming Indian agriculture. *TAAS Bulletin*.
29. Pimentel, D., Hepperly, P., Hanson, J., Douds, D., & Seidel, R. (2005). Environmental, energetic, and economic comparisons of organic and conventional farming systems. *Bioscience, 55*(7), 573–582.
30. Pretty, J., Toulmin, C., & Williams, S. (2006). Sustainable intensification in African agriculture. *International Journal of Agricultural Sustainability, 1*(1), 5–24.
31. Ramesh, P., Panwar, N. R., Singh, A. B., Ramana, D. V., & Yadav, S. K. (2005). Organic farming: Its relevance in India. *Current Science, 88*(4), 561–568.
32. Rodale Institute. (2020). *Regenerative organic agriculture and climate change*. Rodale Institute.
33. Scialabba, N. E., & Müller-Lindenlauf, M. (2010). Organic agriculture and climate change mitigation. *Renewable Agriculture and Food Systems, 25*(2), 158–169.
34. Sharma, A. R., & Behera, U. K. (2009). Recycling of organic wastes in integrated farming systems. *Indian Journal of Agricultural Sciences, 79*(7), 506–511.
35. Singh, R. B., Pal, A. R., & Sinha, S. K. (2000). *Integrated farming systems*. ICAR Publication.
36. Thapa, G., Kumar, A., & Joshi, P. K. (2021). Natural farming in India: Policy and practice. *FAO RAP Publication*.
37. Uphoff, N. (2002). *Agroecological innovations: Increasing food production with participatory development*. Earthscan.
38. Velayutham, M., & Bhattacharyya, T. (2000). Soil resource management for food security and environmental quality. *NBSS LUP Bulletin*.
39. Yadav, A. K., & Chaudhary, R. C. (2014). Organic agriculture in India: Problems and prospects. *Current Science, 106*(4), 525–529.
40. Ziesemer, J. (2007). Energy use in organic food systems. *FAO Natural Resources Management and Environment Department*.
41. IPCC. (2019). *Climate change and land: Summary for policymakers*. Intergovernmental Panel on Climate Change.
42. NITI Aayog. (2021). *Doubling farmers' income by 2022: Strategy document*. Government of India.
43. World Bank. (2006). *India: Inclusive growth and service delivery*. World Bank Report.
44. Just Agriculture Education Group. (2023). *Monthly magazine archives*. Just Agriculture.
45. International Federation of Organic Agriculture Movements (IFOAM). (2014). *IFOAM norms for organic production and processing*. IFOAM.

46. 46.Thapa, G., Kumar, A., & Joshi, P. K. (2021). Natural farming in India: A synthesis and way forward. *IFPRI Discussion Paper 2035*. International Food Policy Research Institute.
47. Tilman, D., Cassman, K. G., Matson, P. A., Naylor, R., & Polasky, S. (2002). Agricultural sustainability and intensive production practices. *Nature, 418*(6898), 671–677. https://doi.org/10.1038/nature01014
48. Uphoff, N. (2002). Agroecological innovations: Increasing food production with participatory development. *Earthscan Publications.*
49. Velayutham, M., & Bhattacharyya, T. (2000). Soil resource management in relation to climate change. *Journal of the Indian Society of Soil Science, 48*(4), 704–716.
50. Walker, B., Holling, C. S., Carpenter, S. R., & Kinzig, A. (2004). Resilience, adaptability and transformability in social–ecological systems. *Ecology and Society, 9*(2), 5.
51. Wezel, A., Bellon, S., Doré, T., Francis, C., Vallod, D., & David, C. (2009). Agroecology as a science, a movement and a practice. *Sustainable Agriculture, 29*(4), 503–515.
52. Wilson, M., & Tisdell, C. (2001). Why farmers continue to use pesticides despite environmental, health and sustainability costs. *Ecological Economics, 39*(3), 449–462.
53. World Bank. (2008). *World development report: Agriculture for development.* Washington, DC: The World Bank.
54. Yadav, A. K., & Panwar, N. R. (2017). Natural farming: Principles and practices. *National Centre of Organic Farming, Ministry of Agriculture.*
55. Zhang, W., Jiang, F., & Ou, J. (2011). Global pesticide consumption and pollution: With China as a focus. *Proceedings of the International Academy of Ecology and Environmental Sciences, 1*(2), 125–144.
56. Zomer, R. J., Bossio, D. A., Sommer, R., & Verchot, L. V. (2017). Global sequestration potential of increased organic carbon in cropland soils. *Scientific Reports, 7*, 15554.
57. Altieri, M. A., & Nicholls, C. I. (2004). Biodiversity and pest management in agroecosystems (2nd ed.). *CRC Press.*
58. Poux, X., & Aubert, P. M. (2018). An agroecological Europe by 2050: Multifunctional agriculture for healthy eating. *IDDRI Study, 9/2018.*
59. Kumar, R., & Shivay, Y. S. (2016). Organic agriculture: A strategy for sustainable agriculture. *Journal of AgriSearch, 3*(1), 1–5.
60. Singh, R. J., & Pal, S. (2014). Organic agriculture research in India: Status, challenges, and policy options. *Indian Journal of Agricultural Economics, 69*(1), 91–107.
61. Verma, A., & Sinha, S. (2020). Impact of organic farming on soil health. *International Journal of Chemical Studies, 8*(3), 2730–2736.
62. Bhattacharyya, P., Chakraborty, G., & Chakrabarti, K. (2011). Long-term effects of organic amendments on soil quality. *Soil Use and Management, 27*(4), 497–505.
63. Desai, S., & Vanneman, R. (2015). Enhancing nutrition through natural farming. *India Human Development Survey.*
64. Doran, J. W., & Zeiss, M. R. (2000). Soil health and sustainability. *Advances in Agronomy, 56*, 1–54.
65. Ghosh, P. K., et al. (2006). Long-term effect of fertilization on soil organic carbon. *Soil Science Society of America Journal, 70*(5), 1520–1530.
66. Pretty, J. (2008). Agricultural sustainability: Concepts, principles and evidence. *Philosophical Transactions of the Royal Society B, 363*(1491), 447–465.

67. Reganold, J. P., & Wachter, J. M. (2016). Organic agriculture in the twenty-first century. *Nature Plants, 2,* 15221.
68. Singh, P., & Kumar, A. (2021). Natural farming as a model for climate resilience. *Journal of Natural Farming, 1*(1), 12–19.
69. Seufert, V., Ramankutty, N., & Foley, J. A. (2012). Comparing the yields of organic and conventional agriculture. *Nature, 485*(7397), 229–232.
70. LaCanne, C. E., & Lundgren, J. G. (2018). Regenerative agriculture: A paradigm shift. *PeerJ, 6,* e4428.
71. Poudel, D. D., et al. (2002). The role of organic farming in climate change mitigation. *Renewable Agriculture and Food Systems, 17*(4), 234–248.
72. Joshi, P. K., et al. (2006). Sustainability and smallholder farming systems in India. *Agricultural Economics Research Review, 19,* 145–154.
73. Kumar, S., & Singh, G. (2018). Soil biodiversity and natural farming. *Indian Journal of Ecology, 45*(Special Issue), 80–85.
74. Schneider, M., & Francis, C. (2005). Marketing locally produced foods: Consumer and farmer opinions in Washington County, Nebraska. *Renewable Agriculture and Food Systems, 20*(4), 252–260.
75. Tripathi, R., Nayak, A. K., & Panda, B. B. (2014). Rice–wheat system productivity and soil health. *Archives of Agronomy and Soil Science, 60*(4), 495–507.
76. Pawar, S. S., & Yadav, S. K. (2021). Natural farming: Concept, prospects and future strategy. *Indian Journal of Agricultural Sciences, 91*(2), 163–170.
77. Dey, A., & Bhagat, R. M. (2004). Long-term impacts of compost and FYM on soil properties. *Journal of the Indian Society of Soil Science, 52*(1), 80–85.
78. Andrews, S. S., Karlen, D. L., & Cambardella, C. A. (2004). Soil quality assessment: A tool for integrated soil management. *Agronomy Journal, 96*(1), 5–11.
79. Pathak, H., & Wassmann, R. (2007). Introducing greenhouse gas mitigation as a development objective in rice-based agriculture. *Agricultural Systems, 94*(3), 826–837.
80. Sharma, R. P., & Prasad, R. (2013). Sustainable agriculture and soil fertility. *Indian Journal of Fertilisers, 9*(11), 84–91.
81. Andrews, S. S., Karlen, D. L., & Cambardella, C. A. (2004). The soil management assessment framework: A quantitative soil quality evaluation method. *Soil Science Society of America Journal, 68*(6), 1945–1962.
82. Rodale Institute. (2020). *The regenerative agriculture and the soil carbon solution.* Retrieved from https://rodaleinstitute.org
83. Fan, S., & Rue, C. (2020). The role of smallholder farms in food and nutrition security. *IFPRI Blog.* https://www.ifpri.org/blog
84. Pathak, H., & Jain, N. (2014). Carbon footprint of Indian agriculture. *Current Science, 107*(7), 1297–1303.
85. FAO. (2019). *Scaling up agroecology to achieve the Sustainable Development Goals.* Food and Agriculture Organization of the United Nations. http://www.fao.org
86. Lal, R. (2004). Soil carbon sequestration impacts on global climate change and food security. *Science, 304*(5677), 1623–1627.
87. Lampkin, N. H. (1990). Organic farming. *Ipswich: Farming Press Books.*
88. Geier, B. (2007). The IFOAM norms and the principles of organic agriculture. In N. Halberg et al. (Eds.), *Global Development of Organic Agriculture: Challenges and Prospects* (pp. 101–112). CABI.
89. Lockie, S., & Halpin, D. (2005). The 'conventionalisation' thesis reconsidered: Structural and ideological transformation of Australian organic agriculture. *Sociologia Ruralis, 45*(4), 284–307.

90. Chander, G., & Mandal, B. (2010). Soil biological health in organic farming. *Indian Journal of Fertilisers, 6*(9), 88–100.
91. Meena, R. P., Meena, V. S., & Meena, R. S. (2016). Natural farming: A way to sustainable agriculture. *Popular Kheti, 4*(4), 92–94.
92. Prasad, R. (2009). Organic farming vis-a-vis modern agriculture. *Current Science, 96*(5), 641–643.
93. Shukla, S. P., & Singh, A. K. (2022). Climate-resilient agriculture: Practices and impacts. *Journal of Agrometeorology, 24*(Special Issue), 1–9.
94. Bhattacharyya, R., et al. (2013). Conservation tillage and organic nutrient sources: Effects on soil carbon pools and productivity. *Soil & Tillage Research, 132*, 49–60.
95. Mäder, P., et al. (2002). Soil fertility and biodiversity in organic farming. *Science, 296*(5573), 1694–1697.
96. International Federation of Organic Agriculture Movements (IFOAM). (2014). *The IFOAM norms for organic production and processing*. Bonn, Germany: IFOAM.
97. Bhatt, B. P., et al. (2021). Natural farming in the Indian Himalayan region: Prospects and challenges. *Journal of Environmental Biology, 42*(2), 228–234.
98. Francis, C. A., Lieblein, G., Gliessman, S. R., Breland, T. A., Creamer, N., Harwood, R., ... & Wiedenhoeft, M. (2003). Agroecology: The ecology of food systems. *Journal of Sustainable Agriculture, 22*(3), 99–118.
99. Giller, K. E., et al. (2009). Conservation agriculture and smallholder farming in Africa: The heretics' view. *Field Crops Research, 114*(1), 23–34.
100. Willer, H., Trávníček, J., Meier, C., & Schlatter, B. (2021). *The World of Organic Agriculture: Statistics and Emerging Trends 2021*. Research Institute of Organic Agriculture FiBL and IFOAM – Organics International.
101. Kristiansen, P., Taji, A., & Reganold, J. P. (Eds.). (2006). *Organic agriculture: A global perspective*. CSIRO Publishing.
102. Singh, K., & Choudhary, O. P. (2020). Natural farming: An emerging concept for sustainable agriculture. *Journal of Pharmacognosy and Phytochemistry, 9*(2), 1634–1639.
103. Kapoor, R., & Sharma, S. (2022). Natural farming: Beyond organic. *Indian Farming, 72*(3), 14–18.
104. Niggli, U., Earley, J., & Ogorzalek, K. (2021). *Sustainability assessment of food and agriculture systems: Organic and agroecological farming*. UNCTAD.
105. Lammerts van Bueren, E. T., Struik, P. C., & Jacobsen, E. (2002). Ecological concepts in organic farming. *Agriculture and Human Values, 19*(1), 39–52.
106. Stockdale, E. A., Shepherd, M. A., Fortune, S., & Cuttle, S. P. (2002). Soil fertility in organic farming systems. *Soil Use and Management, 18*(1), 301–308.
107. Pimentel, D., Hepperly, P., Hanson, J., Douds, D., & Seidel, R. (2005). Environmental, energetic, and economic comparisons of organic and conventional farming systems. *BioScience, 55*(7), 573–582.
108. Shiva, V. (2008). *Soil not oil: Environmental justice in a time of climate crisis*. South End Press.
109. Tuck, S. L., Winqvist, C., Mota, F., Ahnström, J., Turnbull, L. A., & Bengtsson, J. (2014). Land-use intensity and the effects of organic farming on biodiversity. *Nature Communications, 5*, 5151.
110. Badgley, C., Moghtader, J., Quintero, E., Zakem, E., Chappell, M. J., Avilés-Vázquez, K., ... & Perfecto, I. (2007). Organic agriculture and the global food supply. *Renewable Agriculture and Food Systems, 22*(2), 86–108.
111. Pretty, J., Toulmin, C., & Williams, S. (2011). Sustainable intensification in African agriculture. *International Journal of Agricultural Sustainability, 9*(1), 5–24.

112. Bengtsson, J., Ahnström, J., & Weibull, A. C. (2005). The effects of organic agriculture on biodiversity and abundance: A meta-analysis. *Journal of Applied Ecology, 42*(2), 261–269.

113. Uphoff, N., Kassam, A., & Thakur, A. K. (2015). Challenges of increasing water saving and water productivity in the rice sector. *Water Productivity in Agriculture: Limits and Opportunities for Improvement*, 2, 1–25.